SO LONG ..

SO FAR AWAY

Frontispiece: Doushka in the Forbidden City

SO LONG AGO
SO FAR AWAY

A Memory of Old Peking

CECIL LEWIS

LUZAC
ORIENTAL

LUZAC ORIENTAL
46 Great Russell Street, London WC1
1997

ISBN 1 898942 110 HARDBACK
ISBN 1 898942 129 PAPERBACK

British Library Cataloguing-in-Publication Data.
A catalogue record of this book is available
from the British Library.

Printed and bound in Great Britain by
Bookcraft (Bath) Limited,
Midsomer Norton, Somerset

For DOUSHKA

I wish to acknowledge help from Juliet Bredon's *Peking* and Peter Fleming's *The Siege of Peking* in writing this book.

The photographs in this book are from the personal collections of Cecil and Doushka Lewis.

*N*OW, WHEN I OUGHT TO BE DEAD, but somehow or other seem to be still alive, I thought it might be interesting, seeing that I have really nothing else to do, to take a last cruise back into all those golden memories of China that turn up in my books here and there, but which I have never really brought together and remembered as they were. So this is a book about an almost forgotten way of life and wonderful treasures of past days, all destroyed within my lifetime, but of which I can leave a haunting memory of how life was in the Middle Ages of 1920.

Heavens! That's seventy-five years ago when I was a dashing young man about town, jilted by my latest girl friend, broken hearted and miserable, feeling at the end of my world and then suddenly whirled into life by a question: Would you like to go to China?

China! The other end of the world! Inscrutable faces! Secret Societies! Weird writing! On the Road to Mandalay! Mah Jong! Fascinating! Within a week I was eager to set off with all the panache of a great explorer into that mysterious never-never land—the mystic East! To the fairy tales of Dragons, Temples, Gongs and Opium, to Great Walls and Forbidden Cities. In short to the mysterious city of Peking in northern China—and there—of all things —to teach the Chinese to fly!

What it is to be young! To be innocent, callow and just have a moustache coming! To be wildly delighted at the idea of boarding 'le train bleu' from Victoria to Paris! To Paris, where I had never been! To the romantic city of, to me, sexy pin-up dreams on cottage walls in dingy Royal Flying Corps messes on the Somme! To me who had never been south of Amiens in my life! Now, actually to see the Eiffel Tower, the Champs Elysées, the Folies Bergères! Now actually to touch those young ladies and have those long dreamed of orgies with the pin-ups of the war!

But somehow it didn't work out like that. We had to rush across Paris with tin trunks and portmanteaux to catch the southbound express for Venice, and the disappointment of missing Paris evaporated in the breathtaking excitement of actually seeing Venice! Venice! The most wonderful romantic city in the world: the Grand Canal, St Marks, the Bridge of Sighs, Canaletto, Wagner, Browning! Fancy boarding a ship for Peking from Venice! What a contrast! Marvellous!

I am writing rather excitedly, rather out-of-breathily for, as my thoughts dance back over those days, I seem to feel carried away again by the sense of adventure and wonder, a sense of life rushing towards me, of being on the crest of the wave, drunk at having a magical world opening there before me in the scream of the whistle and the first grind of the bogies—going South!! Ah Life! Life!

The Wagon Lit had the bed turned down and the luggage on the rack and the man shouting down the corridor; '*Diner est servi ... servi*'!

Then, lying awake, listening to the wheels, trying to get to sleep and a lost feeling of being nowhere, between things, lying there in a rumbling vacuum of darkness... Then a stop! I pulled back the curtain and looked out. A foaming torrent boiled beside the track. A little goblin in a pointed hood climbed uphill, a gong said sweetly: Pong! Ping pong! What land was this where even trains received melodious invitations to proceed?

At last the dawn! Steps, hurrying down the corridor 'Passports! Passports!' Stamping up and down the platform. Cold. Snow. Breathing Swiss mountain air. Brig. Then the frontier. Now the Simplon Tunnel. Then Domodossola. Italy!

It was almost the end of a long faceless journey I was to make many times between London and Stresa in those glorious years when I lived in my little villa on the far side of the lake. But this first time, ten years earlier, the great drop down to the shores of the Lago Maggiori was a new and heavenly unfolding for me to the sunlit glitter of Italy. The warmth. The open happiness of the shore-side villages seen against blue water, the blessed sunshine after the dreariness of England. But to me something beyond, a sort of call, a certainty that somehow, someday I should return to this wonderland I first saw one morning en route for China.

I remember drinking great gulps of beauty—and great gulps of coffee from big blue cups and scrumptious black cherry jam—as the train wandered slowly along the lake-shore. But then my mind goes blank. I don't remember going through Milan and on through Verona, Padua, Vicenza. I only know it was already dark when we reached Venice.

There are some moments in life which for some reason or other become indelible in the memory. My arrival that evening in Venice is one of them.

I didn't know what to expect. I didn't know the station was right in the city, that you walked off the train into an empty space, a sort of deck and there beyond it was water! A quite broad stretch of water and beyond it dark shadowy buildings, almost no lights and a long mysterious vista of palaces, as I thought of them then, receding into the shadow, and the whole thing lapped, washed with dark, almost motionless water... That was magical enough, but when out of the shadows a gondola slid up towards me, I held my breath! A gondola! That swaying proud swanshead and long slim sliding form, and on it stood upright and somehow commanding, the figure of a man holding an oar, a huge long oar, a gondolier! And the gondolier was waving, actually waving to me! To me! To come aboard!

It was a sort of dream, and a real dream too, to be met and taken to one's hotel with a gondola for a taxi! You soon find out that you can't sit in a gondola. You have to lie back, loll, act being a lord, dream you are a prince being conveyed to a royal audience. Behind you like a sort of guardian, stands the gondolier, erect, watchful—and the whole magic carpet slides in a series of gentle swayings under the sweeps of the oar which is talking to, caressing the dark water.

It is, I suppose, the most romantic, indolent way of travel ever invented and, at the end of a long journey, almost sent me to sleep, so magical, so restful, was the long slow rhythm and the silence of the still Venetian night.

But almost before I could take in the magical vista of the Grand Canal receding between its walls of palaces, our high enquiring prow swung sharply and we shot in deep between two dark walls and started on what was, I imagine, a short cut to my hotel.

It was all suddenly different, silent, secret, even a bit frightening. There was I, alone in a dark city, at the mercy of a huge man who could easily just lean down, cut my throat, steal my luggage, drop me into the canal, and nobody would ever know who I was, where I had come from or where I was going to!

Immediately I was back in the days of the dreadful Doges, the days of vengeance, intrigue, of rival families and feudal revenges, masked bandits, flashing knives and sudden death. Venice became haunted by its past, its prisons, its fleets, its dominion over the seas, right down the Adriatic to the Mediterranean.

There was a huge stentorian cry: Ha! shouted above me. I sat up. My hair prickled. Now what? A long pause... Tension... But it was only my gondolier observing the rules of the road, just blowing his horn, so to speak, warning oncoming traffic beyond the next corner of his approach. But, of course there was nobody. Only the absolute silence of the sleeping city, another vista of houses, their eaves against the night sky, the gulp of the paddle and the magical out-of-this-world feeling of lovers' promises and tragic pledges, of a perfect hiding place for 'this, our journey to no country and to no end'—and only one discreet observer, who would actually even sing to you—if you were in the mood.

How long did it last? I don't know. For me for ever.

We came out at last under the shadow of the Salute, to cross the Grand Canal and reach the landing stage of the hotel. I slept, drunk with fatigue—and wonder.

Cecil Lewis

*M*ORNING IN A STRANGE CITY! Hardly awake. Yawning. Stretching. Stumbling over to the window, drawing the curtains—and then! Ah! How it floods in! The silver dome of the Salute, the silvery water, the silvery ferries and boats, the whole thing seen in the haze of morning sunlight—and then, beyond it, the huge horrid hulk of a two-funnelled ocean liner! The ship which is to carry us to China. What a blot on the landscape!

But it isn't to carry me yet—not for two or three days anyway—and I shall be able to explore! Buy a guidebook! Walk! I thought you had to go everywhere by water; but you can walk! Walk through narrow paved walkways, over humped-back bridges, always with sudden turns, openings, vistas, cafes—and quiet! Not a sound! No horns, no traffic, nobody rushing or shouting: another world!

Then a shadowed passageway, a narrow opening and suddenly! The glorious smile of I suppose the most famous Piazza in the world, with what looks like an oriental palace at the end of it: St Marks!

'St Marks (so a dear friend wrote) is the most mysterious and intimidating structure in the world, a cluster of jewelled caves over an undulating floor, like a petrified sea: here the textures and surfaces have grown unreal, incense-stained marbles glow like tortoiseshell and amber. There are translucent pillars, columns of unknown substances, relics and vestiges of every civilization. The very dust there held in the hand is a compound of precious substances, flakes of gold from decaying marbles.

It looks like a temple of the Grail designed by Klingsor and a blood eating dragon probably lives behind the famous gold altar with its gems and glittering enamels.'

I hardly dare go in under the four bronze horses and the bronze hero striking the hours and then spend the morning basking in palaces and pictures and in the afternoon take a steamer to see the big blue Madonna on the island of Torcello.

A couple I had casually met over lunch told me they were going to the Opera that evening—and would I care to join them? It was the idea of going to the opera in a gondola that tempted me as much as the music. But sliding through the night canals put us all in a mood of gaiety and romance I shall never forget.

The entrance to the opera house, La Fenice, was well lit and busy with a dozen other parties all arriving alongside together in a queue of gondolas and pouring out a crowd of high spirited young people who set the scene for the most memorable opera performance I ever attended.

The theatre was a pretty period house, small, well shaped, softly lit and full of talkative Italians. But the programme told me that the opera was an obscure piece by Mascagni of whom I had never heard. Its title was *Il Tiratore*, which meant I was told 'marksman' and the plot was, as far as I could make out, some quarrel between two marksmen over a girl. It was all a bit slow and long-winded till towards the end of the second act when the 'hero' sharpshooter had to bring down a passing bird or lose the girl. It was, of course, all bow and arrow stuff. Then came the top note of the big aria. The hero let fly his arrow and, to roars of applause, a large bird fell dead, mid stage.

This stopped the show. The wild applause continued. I saw, to my amazement, that the bird was being hauled off into the wings on a string. Was the number going to be repeated? In an opera, impossible! But this was Italy. Encore! Encore! What the public wanted was that top 'C' to tickle their spines. And here it came, the crescendo, the tenor with bursting veins, then the top note, the arrow and the poor dejected bird falling again, dead, on cue. I have never enjoyed an opera more in my life.

Well I could go on all day about Venice, the churches, the palaces, the pictures, the endless enchantment of it all; but we are bound for China. Getting there, in those days, was a tedious journey, a long haul of six weeks! Six weeks on board a ship—another life in itself!

The Santa Maria was an Italian passenger liner of about 20,000 tons burden, plying regularly between Venice and Tokyo three times a year. She was not luxurious, but had good Italian cooking, comfortable cabins and pottered around the world at about 15 knots. Of course the very idea of a world cruise was to me, at that age and that time, an adventure. Every port was a new encounter, a new experience, and I looked forward to it all with the eagerness and gusto of my age. But at the end of the trip—well the best I could say of the Santa Maria was that she got us there.

In 1920 although the war had been over two years international traffic was only just getting back into gear. The passengers were of all nationalities, odd business men, families emigrating, people going back to their pre-war occupations wondering how relatives or businesses had fared over the four years or more they had been away. So you heard many languages and for quite a time customs, habits and food needed getting used to. It took people some time to settle down.

Air travel today is just a waiting room—a pause between destinations. But a long journey is a fascinating life in itself with all its complications, quarrels, intrigues, affairs and crises that occur between strangers herded up together in cooped-up conditions for sometimes a week or more at a time.

I remember nothing of our trip down the Adriatic and our first stop at Alexandria, nor of the Suez canal, the Dead Sea, and Aden where the first of our passengers disembarked, officers and men rejoining their units in the British Garrison there.

But at Aden the first heat struck us. Now we were really into shipboard life. We began to sweat, cast off clothing and live in shirts, shorts and sandals. From now on it was going to be life in the tropics all the way to Shanghai.

Our next stop was Colombo and here, for me, the magic of the journey began. Tropical seas and palm groves make poetry into prose for today's tourists. But for me they were the wonder they still are for those who can really look and see. The actual beauty of the Sinhalese took me by storm. I still think the Indian people have a grace, suavity and charm surpassing all others. The first impressions of Colombo, the hands joined in greeting, the men's turbans, the girls' saris and smiles, the whole scene flooded with a new kind of feeling, the sense of another way of life, based on something sacred coming from the remote past. All this left memories for a lifetime.

I remember passing a small booth in a market square where there were jars of semi-precious stones and a smiling bearded man standing there who actually had this treasure for sale, pouring a cupful of moonstones into my cupped hands! I remember the hot curries, the mangoes, the tea and the diamond light washing everything with happiness and peace—lost, alas, to us all today.

Then we were off again into the second leg of our crossing of the Indian Ocean. Next stop, Penang, in those days a small fishing village on the northern shore of the Malay Peninsula. Before us six days of nothing to the four horizons but the endless emptiness of the Indian Ocean.

One of my ways to escape the monotony of the days was to clamber up to the prow of the ship and stand there, in our 15 knot breeze, 'monarch of all I surveyed'. I loved the boiling white divided scroll of the sea cut by the prow, the continual hiss of the foam and feeling the morning, there, alone, overlooking the great ocean.

Occasionally came a surprise skittering sound, a flying fish surfacing out of our way and skimming off low over the water; but better, the glorious morning greeting from schools of dolphins, leaping and diving together either side of the prow, bringing such a sense of freedom, laughter and happiness—and such a loss of good company when they left us to plunge back into their own mysterious life.

Looking behind me up to the bridge I sometimes waved to the officer of the watch, who saw these morning meditations of mine or to the Captain who always gave me a friendly wave. I felt a certain sympathy with them. This trip, which was a big adventure to us, was just the repetition of a routine to them. The passengers were no great stimulus either. Most of them didn't speak Italian. I had quickly tired of attempts at conversation with my limited French and German. I felt, very stupidly, that, being English, I was superior. Today I see how vain and stupid that was. They must all have had interesting stories to tell. They had uprooted their lives, gone abroad to live with strangers, made their homes in lonely, sometimes dangerous places. What was so special about me? My interest was even less than theirs— just the lady next door.

She had tapped, very quietly, very gently on the thin partition between our cabins. Thinking she might be in some difficulty or distress, I went in to find she was indeed in distress, but with a malady for which I happened to have a remedy handy. The distress turned out to be recurrent and so we agreed it would be wise to continue the treatment until the end of the voyage.

I had already been thinking up a way to escape the boredom of the long voyage. The next stop after Penang was Singapore, another four day stretch. But, looking at the map, it seemed actually quite a short distance and—excitement and surprise— there was actually a railway between the two places! A train would make the journey far quicker than the ship, so why not take the train, see Malaysia and have a real holiday, free from the disapproving eyes and cramped conditions of cabin life?

Our stop at Colombo had been marvellous, our first view of the tropics, golden beaches, waving palms, exotic food, but all very tidy, picture-postcard stuff. As we came in to moor at Penang, we got quite a different feeling. Wild, simple, little fishing houses sticking up, on stilts, with boats moored underneath. The shore seemed narrow and beyond, rising over low hills, a solid green backing of tropical forest, the jungle! The jungle! Magic word! That meant monkeys, lions and tigers, boa-constrictors, Treasure Island, Robinson Crusoe and the Blue Lagoon!

Of course it was a crazy thing to do. We might never get to Singapore, how often did the trains run, what would it cost, could we do it in the time, the ship would leave without us! All that sort of stuff. But we didn't care. We had it all planned. I had a word with the Captain. He was a man of the world. He just laughed, nodded, clapped his hand on my shoulder and called 'Sta felice! Buon viaggio!' as we positively bounced down the gangplank and made for the train!

The train! If the magic hadn't started already, it started there. It was a toy train—with a rail gauge of about three feet, an engine all red paint and brass polish and coaches to match. I felt if you wanted you could just pick it all up, turn it round and put it back on the rails again and go the other way!

And when we got going! The engine was evidently wild about itself! It clanked, snorted, blew its toy whistle, puffed clouds of white smoke and was obviously shouting to the world at large. 'Look! Here I go! I'm off! Why not join me? Cheery oh! See you later!'

But it was all well kept, spotlessly clean and the Guard when he came to take our tickets, saluted and beamed, 'Good day, Sah! Thank you Sah!' as if we were no less than royalty!

The track itself was far from perfect. There were bumps and joggles and continuous steady rocking which gave us vague feelings of sea sickness or worse, that our journey might come to an end without notice.

In the carriage you sat lengthwise. If you had slept across, your feet would have stuck out into the jungle! And our sleeping berth! I shall never forget. It too lay lengthwise, very narrow. When we managed to arrange ourselves on it and, so to speak, get into position, it proved quite unnecessary to make any further efforts. The train took care of all that automatically. We called it randy rocking and it set us laughing till we managed to get off to sleep.

How we got to Kuala Lumpor and found a hotel I can't remember. But I do remember the room. It was such a contrast to the train, a huge airy tropical room with high ceilings, big French windows and a view down over the grounds, shady trees and white seats! After our cabins and that train, this was luxury!

But there were funny things about it. The door, for instance, was open, top and bottom, you couldn't close it. Fine for air circulation—but not for privacy. If there were any wild shrieks of delight, which sometimes overcome young people in the night, everybody would hear. I remembered how back home (at Marlow) one night, our ecstasies had actually called in the night staff to see if we were 'all right'. We told them that we were.

Then there were those curtains carefully hung at the head of the bed. What could they be? Mosquito nets, suggested the young lady. Of course! But I had never seen one before. How did they work? Well, let me tell all non-tropicalities, beware! They spell trouble to the innocent. They are very light and thin.

14

They float about in the air. They never seem to hang as they should. You hear the brutes buzzing away outside, but if, by bad luck, one gets INSIDE! Then! You try to catch it, swot it, make a hole in the net and then, goodbye to a peaceful night!

But the last and most glorious surprise in our bedroom was the bath! It wasn't a bath, it was a huge tub, a sort of urn, like you see at Knossos, over four feet high and wide open at the top. I remember it as being made of earthenware, but it may just have been wood, a stout tall wooden barrel, full of cold water! It stood alone, like an altar, at the centre of an open space, inviting splashing and all sorts of romps.

In fact it makes a fitting picture to end the memory of our Malaysian honeymoon. The sunlit early morning room. The lovely young lady, very neat and small, up to her shoulders in the tub, her arms wide, shouting and about to throw her sponge at me, and I, laughing and leaping at her, lifting her clean out of the tub into my arms.

꿈: ꙉ

I'd always had a feeling about Singapore. I looked forward to seeing it. Somehow I knew it was a vibrant, exciting and energetic city. Perhaps it was because it stood on the main junction of the seas and continents of our world. Just the word, Singapore, had a lucky sound about it. Certainly since those early days it had grown and flourished into having its own special place in the world.

The Santa Maria had dutifully just arrived to greet us and we went aboard, met several of our ship passengers and decided to go out together and find somewhere to eat in the city. You could feel at once it was brimming with life!

We were taken to a popular, well known restaurant, very gay and prosperous. The tables were all out in the open but shaded right down to the pavement and ours happened to be quite near the kerb, on the edge of the street. There was a lot going on, people passing, all ages, all colours, a sunlit picture of vigorous life and movement.

Without my noticing it a passer-by had put down his basket on the edge of the kerb next to me and was kneeling before it, introducing himself to me with joined hands, bowing and making signs of welcome. He looked very poor, a beggar probably, with something to sell. I leaned forward with a smile, and he bowed and took the cloth off the top of his basket.

I sat back very hastily. In the basket were two snakes! And these snakes I saw at once were no nice ordinary English garden snakes, they had strange markings and a sort of menace in their movements. Taking off the cover admitted light and the two creatures at once reared up, displaying their long leaf-like hoods with bullet-like heads above darting eyes and sudden shooting tongues. From my school picture books I recognised them at once. They were cobras, hooded cobras! Gosh!

The fellow, who owned these obvious dangers to public safety, was sitting quietly smiling, obviously delighted at the effect of his pets. One of our party who knew the form said: 'He just wants to make them dance for you.'

You smile at my innocence and fright because you have seen all this kind of thing on TV. But in 1920, Hooded Cobras! Loose, in the street! Well I, at any rate, didn't expect to be suddenly confronted by that sort of thing at short range and treat it as a matter of course. I didn't know how to react. The best thing I thought was to sit still and be ready to bolt in emergency.

Meanwhile this chap had pulled a sort of penny whistle out of his sleeve and had begun to play music to these lethal pets of his. He played very quietly, very carefully, as though he wasn't quite sure himself if they weren't about to make a dive at him with those black darting tongues. In fact having reared themselves well up over the top of the basket, they began to sway to and fro as if mesmerized. This swaying began to mesmerize me too. It was most beautiful to watch and the interweaving delicacy of their slim, dance-like movements seemed to evoke a fascinating peace that came over me and their master. Even the other onlookers seemed rivetted, as if we all expected something to happen. But nothing did. After a bit more swaying and one or two ineffectual darts towards him, their master changed the tune on his whistle and the two poor creatures, somehow jaded, sank back into their basket and were covered up. We made a hasty collection, he got up, put our coppers into a bag, smiled, bowed low to us and disappeared.

Of course all this gave rise to a lot of excited conversation. Those who had seen it before smiled knowingly, others covered up, taking it as a matter of course, my young lady was scared and said so. So was I—at first, but then I began to be astonished. These were wild creatures. They had been caught, fed, found to be mesmerized by music, tamed to live in a basket and had been straightaway seen as a commercial asset, carted off to the city to earn coppers on the pavement. How poor people must be to have to live like this!

Before we had time to talk much about this we were served food. Lovely curry and—I remember vividly—some pink bananas! I had never tasted pink bananas before, and never have tasted them since, but they were delicious and are one of my best Singapore memories.

I only realized later that the restaurant was privy to this kind of street entertainment when a waiter, taking away my plate, nudged me and half whispered, pointing: 'That man— magic man. Very good.'

I feel I must make it quite clear I was there in all these scenes. I am not making it up. All this took place on a busy Singapore street in broad hot tropical daylight. We were confronted by a tall, rather imposing, bearded man. With him were two other young men and a boy. They were all dressed in rather dirty long white garments and carried a large wicker basket, the size of a small trunk, which they put down on the ground before them.

The bearded man obviously knew quite well that we were strangers off the ship and went into his act with all the assurance of a professional.

'All ladies, gentlemans, good days! I, Master Magician! I take this boy, my son'—and he took the boy by the shoulders and lifted his dhobi off over his head—'he good boy. You touch him. He no dummy.' He pushed the boy towards us, keeping up a line about his years of mystical study, his magical power to cast spells. Now, to show us how powerful these spells were, he would shut his own son in this trunk and '...If my spells fail, I will kill him with my sword!' and he produced a long sharp sword and whirled it above his head. At the same time his two assistants were showing off an ordinary wicker trunk, turning it this way and that, opening it, showing its lid, hinges, the strap that went round it and so on.

'Now,' the Magician went on, 'You,' pointing at me, 'You touch the boy. He not dummy.' The boy came towards me—he was now naked except for a pair of pants—he turned a couple of cart-wheels and held out his hand. I shook it. He was a nice young smiling boy. I suppose about eight or nine years old.

Meanwhile the other two young men had opened the trunk on the road and the boy, first looking up at his father's sword seriously, went over and crouched down, just able to squeeze into it. The Magician made a vigorous sign, the young men slammed the lid down, closed the lid strap and invited me to come and lift the trunk to make sure the boy was inside it. I went over and tried to lift it. Certainly he, or something heavy, was inside it.

Then the hocus-pocus started. As far as I can recall, it was a sort of chant danced round the trunk, absolutely serious and somehow rather impressive. They made as if to lift it, felt its weight, with the Magician standing over it, whirling his sword, and uttering weird—and somehow rather terrifying—cries. After a few moments of this, suddenly, the Magician shouted a tremendous order! 'Boy! Go!'

Immediately he drove his sword straight down through the lid of the trunk and left it shaking there. Not satisfied with this he pulled out the sword and drove it through the sides, the ends, then top again, as if to make it quite clear there was nothing alive inside it. Then, with a grand wave, he ordered his men to open the trunk. It was quite empty.

Of course it was a trick. We all knew that. But it was, after all, pretty impressive, done on the roadside with all Singapore passing, stopping to watch. There were plenty of locals who could have given him away, laughed at him. But nobody did. We all cheered and clapped, while the Magic Man smiling and obviously pleased with himself, came and shook hands, offered his brass plate into which we contributed liberally, rather dazed by the whole thing, so unexpected, so unusual.

Then, to cap it all, the boy suddenly reappeared, delighted to see everybody, smiling and, of course, offering his own brass plate. Finally the head waiter appeared with his plate—which we met in sterling, none of us having had time to change money into Singaporian currency. So the city did well out of us, but we did well out of it, carrying away memories never to be repeated in a lifetime.

The Singapore stop was the climax of our voyage. After it Hong Kong, though we arrived there at an important moment, left a far less impressive memory.

The fact that it was part of the British Empire was, of course, important to us. To find English spoken, see English signs, drive on the left of the road, find everything neat and tidy, all this we accepted as normal, the way to do things. The people were Chinese of course, another race, but they were obviously far better off, learning English ways, living under English laws and, above all, speaking the English language.

Our other stops had been different, exciting, strange; but, compared with Hong Kong, they all seemed hopelessly unorganized, untidy, poverty stricken. Hong Kong was neat, clean, orderly, prosperous, part of the empire ' upon which the sun never sets', the greatest civilizing influence the earth had ever seen. Britain was way out ahead, as usual, and we were proud of it.

Our arrival happened to coincide with a world cruise being made by our latest craze, that pride of princely prodigy, Edward, Prince of Wales. He was doing a world tour of token service with HMS *Renown*, flagship of the Royal Navy, and the whole island was lit up in his honour. The Peak, a prosperous hillside overlooking the harbour, glowed with hundreds of red lanterns at night. We could hear distant music. The whole island was having a ball.

Fortunately we did not see then that England had bled itself to death in the empty victory of World War I and that from that time on its glory would steadily diminish, its influence, wealth and empire disintegrate, leaving even its greatest gift to civilization, its English language, eroded into a cacophony of computerism. We were living, as it is said, in a fool's paradise—probably every generation is!

But now we were nearing the end of our voyage, the Santa Maria would put down most of her passengers at Shanghai and take on a few more, bound for her final destination, Tokyo.

My neat, gay little companion of the voyage seemed sad and somehow lost when we parted. Our chance meeting had certainly made the voyage for me. Now I was going on to exciting days ahead. And she?

Was she really going to a husband in Japan, as she had said? I wondered. It was best not to enquire.

'I shall never forget our days together,' she said. I held her to me.

'I too!' It was true. But words are no good for endings. I have kept her in my memory, in my books—over many years—a gulp of pure happiness—seventy years ago!

What happened to her? I shall never know...

Even in those days Shanghai was a developed seaport, the main entrance to China through which most of the world entered that vast and unknown country. But Shanghai was not our entrance. We had to change ships and steam northwards for another thousand miles to a smaller port, Tientsin and even then take a train for a hundred miles more to reach our Mecca, the city of Peking itself.

By this time I was tired of travelling. The distances seemed endless. We had come half around the world after all. Of all this last stopping, waiting about, changing ships and lugging our luggage onto the final train, I remember nothing at all.

But the final picture is clear. The old train, with its huge exhausted engine, finally lugged itself into Peking station and came to rest practically touching the towering southern Wall of Peking itself. This was our Mecca. Practically no lights, the platform crowded with porters, passengers, shouting, smoke. We clasped hands with strangers who had come to meet us. We had arrived. It was just like Paddington.

*T*HERE MUST, I FEEL, HAVE BEEN some guiding hand that booked me into that room on the fourth floor of the Hotel de Pekin, the latest and best hotel in the city of Peking.

We were feeling very relaxed and contented to have, at last, reached journey's end and had enjoyed a hearty, rather noisy, welcoming supper with the family who represented Vickers Ltd, the company that had sent us here. In fact it had been such a hearty party that I remember making the journey back to our hotel, sitting (and singing) astride the bonnet of their car.

Somehow or other I got to my room and woke up late next morning after my first really sound sleep for six weeks and lay there in bed, trying to realize that I had at last reached the city of my dreams, but had no idea where my hotel stood, nor any idea of where my room was in it. But at last it slowly entered my aching head that I might look out of the window and see. So I got up, pulled the curtains, opened the windows and pushed back the shutters.

It was one of those moments when your eyes do not believe what they are seeing. There, right below me and before me lay the whole Forbidden City!

It lay there in the morning sun, golden roof upon golden roof, courtyard after courtyard, braided with red walls, white marble stairways and terraces, the eye slowly becoming aware of the whole as of some huge golden maze, laid out by a magician, secrecy within secrecy, wall within wall, each graced with its own small palace. And, at the centre of it all, on a terrace above the rest, the Throne Room itself, the audience chamber, the holy of holies, a glittering golden solitaire, the Throne of the Emperor.

As I write this, piling superlative on superlative, after seeing this same marvellous view, morning after morning, every day of my life for several months, I must add that the first impression of magnificence began to grow more and more sad. The City was an empty shell. There was nobody in it—except, it was said, beyond the last northern doorway into the most secret courtyard—where there lived a young boy of sixteen, the heir to the throne of China, never permitted to speak or to be seen, kept , like a caged pet, studying with an English tutor, to inherit the throne he would never rule.

But to me, as to anyone living in Peking in those days, the City was not at all Forbidden. I spent many hours wandering through its courtyards, touching these endless balustrades, feeling the cool of white marble, trying to sense how the craftsmen must have felt when they fashioned these wonders, pausing in doorways to taste the beauty of the vista beyond, looking up to marvel at the sweep of the great upcurling roofs, a mystery of craftsmanship in themselves.

If the Forbidden City, dying there before my eyes, became for me a forlorn wonder, it was also the most perfect monument to a glorious past that I have ever seen. The Chinese do not build large impressive memorials to power or holiness, as we do in the West. The scale of their building is always based on wood. The limit of their scale is set by the size of the biggest tree trunk they can make into a column. But they have developed a unique and striking sense of scale, an awe-inspiring feeling of calm and peace—by the master stroke of emptiness.

Those perfect courtyards, those noble terraces, that unique beauty of line and form stood there basking, a dying memorial of wonder, born out of laws, traditions, a deep respect for the past and the hope of a glorious future. But the huge sprawling monster of China could never be administered as a whole and finally, like Russia, fell to pieces.

∿∴∾

I was due at 8.30 a.m. to meet all the people at the 'office' and get to know them and the general lie of the land. But how to get there? I'd been told, 'Just say "Office, Vickers." to the Hall Porter and he'll get you a rickshaw.'

The Hall Porter, of course, knew everybody in the city, who they were and where they lived. He called a rickshaw and waved me off to the residence of my hosts, Vickers Ltd.

But a rickshaw! This was another adventure, like everything else since I left Victoria. I had never seen a rickshaw before. It looked like some mobile armchair. I got in nervously and felt the 'boy'—that is my human horse—lift the shafts and calmly trot me off! It was an absolutely new sensation. The thing had rubber tyres, springs, and a very comfortable seat. Rickshaws were simply solo luxury travel!

The fact that mine was powered by a laughing young man who seemed to be able to trot for ever worried me. I didn't like the idea of it; but I very soon saw: this was how it was.

It was Peking's morning rush hour. The whole city seemed to be on wheels! Thousands of rickshaws were trotting about—and every one had his 'horn', a bicycle bell—and every boy was ringing it! It was a riot, a chorus of bells, the most jubilant rush hour I was ever in.

There was a bit of other traffic—carts with gay blue canvas covers, big wheels and mules, diminutive black shiny carriages, very posh and superior, powered by huge Australian horses, called whalers—but most outlandish were the occasional local omnibus, a cart drawn by an assortment of animals all loosely roped together in a team, mule, donkey, pony, even a cow.

Beside them the driver, without reins or whip, shouting streams of totally unprintable language and, somehow or other getting the animals to pull the cart—and the passengers who, for some unimaginable reason were reduced to travelling in it. But the rickshaw was the Peking taxi and made the show. The whole thing was a sort of *musical medieval traffic jam* and, sitting there, goofing at the glorious gaiety of it all, I found I was laughing. It was crazy, it was ridiculous, it was gorgeous! This was my first day in Peking! This was life!

When I got to the 'office', we chatted in a very relaxed way about our trip, met other members of the staff and the Chinese 'Compradore'—a key figure, as I was later to find out, our contact with the Chinese authorities, our go-between in all negotiations—and our interpreter—for nobody on the staff spoke fluent Chinese. I was given a brief idea of the Chinese way of doing business, the importance of 'squeeze', the rake-off that go-betweens expected and were entitled to and so on. Then we got onto the 'men', that is the team of mechanics who were to erect and service the aeroplanes, were they all right? where would they live? etc. Then it was the bank, money, shopping. But in the middle of this the Tai-Tai, that is, in Chinese, the Lady of the House, butted in.

'The first thing you have to do is to drop cards.'

'Drop cards?'

'Yes. You have to be introduced to the Peking Society. The Legation, the Army, the Diplomatic Corps, everybody wants to get to know you, to entertain you, so theoretically you have to pay them all polite visits to introduce yourself. But that would take ages so—have you got any visiting cards?'

'No, I'm afraid I don't go in for...'

'Doesn't matter. It's just a formality. I'll get some cards done for you. We'll do the rounds ... I'll come with you. We just have to choose the time—when everybody's out or resting. Then we drop in the card and hop it. If we're lucky we'll get through ten or more in one afternoon and finish off the less important ones the next day…'

I was genuinely alarmed. I knew nothing about social graces. Society scared me.

'Must we?'

'Yes. Absolutely. Vickers has quite a standing here you know. Big contracts with the Chinese; Trams, Transport, Railways and, of course, aircraft. Flying is something new. Everybody wants to meet you!'

So, eventually, we dropped cards. As a result we met one or two 'important' people, who sized me up, labelled me, got me into the Club and made polite noises; but I soon found out what a cracking bore the whole thing was.

Here in the capital of the oldest civilization in the world, whose beauty and antiquity were breath-taking, these superior 'foreigners' went from office to club, from tennis to cocktails, from dinner to bridge, and from bridge to bed. Some of them rode or took a fortnight's picnic holiday in the hot weather at one of the many deserted Temples outside the city. But most of them looked down on the Chinese as dirty, uneducated and untrustworthy, while the Chinese lumped us altogether as 'foreign devils'.

I wanted none of this. I had come to China to meet the Chinese and work with them. I wasn't interested in the golf course and the Club. Even after a few hours I already felt fascinated by everything Chinese. Later I found many among the young who felt as I did.

⌣∶∾

The business of 'dropping cards' to which I had been introduced on the first morning after our arrival turned out to be a very good way to get the feel of the city and the lie of the chief landmarks, while on our way to the Legation Quarter.

I assumed that this imperative need to drop cards would be to make ourselves known to our hosts, the Chinese. But it soon turned out nobody had the least intention of doing anything like that. During my whole time in China I was never presented or introduced to our hosts—and employers—the Chinese Government nor met any high ranking officer in the projected Chinese Air Force.

I got to know quite a lot of young men who hoped to be pilots and occasionally somebody who looked after them. But it seemed as though the Chinese authorities felt they ought to have an air force, but knew nothing about it and so must 'order' one from abroad. Hence our presence in Peking. In those days China was not a nation, but she assumed, when powerless, the place of the world power she was destined to become.

The Chinese did not then, or now, accept the western way of life, considering, as we all do, that their own way was far better. However, after some ineffectual rebellions and risings at the turn of the century to rid herself of 'the hated foreigners', China was obliged to accept their existence and accommodate herself to their demands. This resulted in the founding and setting up of an area in their city where these intruders could live freely to make their own laws and live in their own way. From it western influences began to have an influence on the whole development of China.

So, in a sort of shouted conversation between trotting rickshaws I gathered there was a whole world of foreign interests in Peking, that nearly all western nations had their representatives in the city and nearly all were housed together in the Legation Quarter.

But it was not even with other nations, the smart French, the charming Scandinavians or the Russian Bear we were to meet, it was the (then) greatest power of all, the British, the nice, decent, ordinary 'diplomatic' servants of the British Empire that demanded our attention.

By the time I got there, about twenty years after the 'troubles' had been settled, the Legation Quarter was already a small thriving international village within the Chinese capital, with its own local laws, its own guards, its own roads and regulations, its own post office, shops and police and even its own excellent hotel, Les Wagon Lits.

The Legations themselves were immediately recognizable from the rest of the city, being built like the large town houses in the European architecture of the period, with surrounding gardens, stout walls and iron gates.

However the British Legation was itself quite different from all others, being originally a palace given by an Emperor to his thirty-third son! The British restored it to its original style, but somehow gave it a pleasant country house air, an imposing Chinese looking Ministry and, as you might expect, it being our national instinct, a beautiful garden. The property was originally leased from the Chinese for a yearly fee of £500. The sum, in silver ingots, being conveyed regularly every year for forty years by the Minister's Secretary to the Yamen in a mulecart!

These outposts of western governments were not a close happy community, any more than they are today, but they needed each other and managed a compromise, the father of it all being, much to my surprise, the Russians. China and Russia have a common border, had been in touch with each other long before the West had made its entrance and had established good friendly relations, concessions and even set up their own religion, a little church in the city itself—in which, a little later, I was to be married!

꒦꒦

The inspiring view of the Forbidden City from my fourth floor window was, in fact, a view forbidden to every Chinese in the old days. Nobody dared even to think of looking down on the

Emperor! Even the guards on the city walls were ordered never to look behind them. So I was seeing a view few Chinese saw, even in my day. The superb view was over the last and most magnificent of these walled cities, of which the ruins of at least four others could still be found nearby.

Records of China go back into the remote prehistoric days of over 2,000 BC when the first settlers saw the district of Yen as being 'a very pleasant land of streams, lakes and fish, where roam deer, elephants, tigers and bears.' It is said these early Chinese invented the wheel, the boat, the plough and the city as a 'walled place with gates and a palace'.

History records show that nine Dynasties preceded the ruined city of Tang Sovereigns who reigned in Peking from AD 618 to BC 907. This period is still known as The Golden Age of Chinese Learning, though Lao Tzu, Confucius and Mencius are said to have lived at least 500 years before that.

Peking has been the site of these walled cities. They were built centuries apart, the walls often touching each other, but they can still be seen on the map to be separate enclaves.

So Peking became a god-given spot on the earth's surface. For three thousand years they built these perfect square cities set, almost like tombs, precisely in the same direction. The roots of China must always be here. It was a divine command given by their ancestors.

Incidentally China, in my day even, never used the words 'left' or 'right'. They invented the compass and always used it to give directions. When I was looking for my lost ball on the golf course, my caddy at once cried: 'To the north, the north. Now west, a little to the west … . Now, a step south. There!'

From my window I could see part of the huge South Wall of Peking. Even at first glance that morning I felt its weight and protection. In those days all four walls were still standing. Beside them The Forbidden City itself seemed small, a hidden heart, a huge royal residence for the Emperor and his retinue of family, relatives and hangers-on. Outside its two miles of walls lay an unwalled area reserved to princes, nobles and dignitaries, known as the Imperial City. Beyond this again lay the Great Walls of Peking itself, The City of Nine Gates.

Later, I began to feel Peking as a symbol, the focus of an age-old way of life, a life of high morality, filial piety and devotion to their living god, the Son of Heaven. Hidden by cities within cities, walls within walls, their Emperor dwelt in the Throne Room and was seated alone, upon the Throne itself, the Ruler of the World.

The great city, over ten miles square, was wholly reserved to his citizens, the people of Peking, but a large part of it remained unbuilt on, a countryside of streams and meadows. Outsiders, 'foreigners' from other parts of China, of other blood, were consigned to what is now called the Chinese City, a huge over-crowded area of markets and theatres, of shops and slums, which lies immediately outside the South Wall. It was against this wall that our train had steamed in when we arrived. 'Firewagons' were not allowed within the City. But to me this Chinese City became the most attractive part of Peking. It was intensely alive, exciting, interesting. Here the life of the city lay. The Forbidden City was an antique, derelict.

Aerial picture of the Forbidden City

*T*HE earliest personal record of the mythical City of Peking occurs in the thirteenth century accounts of the great traveller, Marco Polo, describing what he saw:

> Now there was on that spot in old times a great and noble city called Cambaluc, which is as much as to say in our tongue 'The City of the Emperor'...
>
> As regards the size of this city you must know that it hath a compass of 24 miles, for each side of it hath a length of six miles and it is four square. And it is all walled round with walls of earth which have a thickness of ten paces at the bottom, and a height of more than ten paces: but they are not so thick at the top for they diminish in thickness as they rise so that at the top they are only about three paces thick. And they are provided throughout with loop-holed battlements which are all whitewashed.
>
> The streets are so straight and wide that you can see right along them end to end and from one gate to the other. And up and down the city there are beautiful palaces and many great and fine hostelries and fine houses in great numbers. (All the plots of ground on which the houses of the city are built are four square and laid out with straight lines, all the plots being occupied by great and spacious palaces with courts and gardens of proportionate size. All these plots were assigned to different heads of families. Each square plot is encompassed by handsome streets for traffic and thus the whole city is arranged in squares just like a chessboard, and disposed in a manner so perfect and masterly that it is impossible to give a description that should do it justice.)

Moreover in the middle of the city there is a great clock—that is to say a bell—which is struck at night. And after it had struck three times nobody must go out in the city except for the needs of a woman in labour or of the sick. And those who go about on such errands are bound to carry lanterns with them. Moreover the established guard at each gate of the city is one thousand armed men, not that you are to imagine this guard is kept for fear of any attack, but only as a guard of honour for the Sovereign who resides there and to prevent thieves from doing mischief in the town.

You must know that here is the greatest Palace that ever was. The Palace itself hath no upper storey but is all on the ground floor, only the basement is raised some ten palms above the surrounding soil and this elevation is retained by a wall of marble raised to the level of the pavement two spaces in width and projecting beyond the base of the Palace so as to form a kind of terrace-walk by which people can pass round the building, whilst on its outer edge there is a very fine pillared balustrade and up to this the people are allowed to come. The roof is very lofty, and the walls of the Palace are all covered with gold and silver. They are also adorned with representations of dragons (sculptured in gilt), beast and birds, knights and idols and sundry other subjects. And on the ceiling too, you see nothing but gold and silver and painting. (On each of the four sides there is a great marble staircase leading to the top of the marble wall and forming the approach to the Palace.)

The Hall of the Palace is so large that it could easily dine six thousand people and it is quite a marvel to see how many rooms there are besides. The building is altogether so vast, so rich and so beautiful that no man on earth could design anything superior to it. The outside of the roof is all coloured with vermilion and yellow and green and blue and other hues which are fixed with varnish so fine and exquisite that they shine like crystal and lend a resplendent lustre to the Palace as seen from a great way around. The roof is made too with such strength and solidity that it is fit to last for ever.

~:~

The City of Nine Gates, as Peking used to be called, has indeed nine gates, two on the North wall, two on the West wall and two on the East wall, but the South wall has three gates, the centre one, the imposing Ch'ien Men, being the main gate, the front door, so to speak, of Peking.

The whole city is planned with architectural accuracy. The discovery of the Magnetic Meridian at a time when China was emerging from the Dark Ages came to them as a divine revelation. Hidden, but running through all life, as a pointer, a direction, that must be obeyed. From it they developed the compass which became a lifeguide in building their cities, their roads, their temples and houses, all obedient to this sense of a divine order in life. Peking is the prototype of correct living by this sacred principle.

So the architects laid out the position of the gates on the West wall exactly matching their place on the East wall. The two gates on the North wall and the three on the South exactly divide those walls into three or four equal lengths. This meticulous accuracy extends to the inner layout of the city where all small streets, or 'hutungs' as they are called, are all laid out north–south or east–west. It is a great help in getting about the maze of the city—and foreshadows, after all, the modern systems of 'grid' building by a few thousand years.

As a practical system of defence I don't think walls are of much use, they are always penetrated. But in peacetime they give a wonderful sense of protection against wars to come! When they are built on the magnificent scale of the Peking walls, they feel quite impregnable.

To get some idea of their size you have to climb up and stand on top of them. They measure more than the height of a two-storey house and on their flat top you could march twelve men abreast. This gives a massive scale to the city and when every gate in the wall is surmounted by a huge gatehouse, the quarters of the guard that used to man the wall, the general effect is very impressive and gives a sense of grandeur to all the palaces and temples within the city.

It was forbidden to walk the walls in the days when I was there, but a length near the Legation Quarter had been opened to foreigners as a place to stretch their legs. The streets were too busy and dusty to do much walking and this made a welcome retreat to enjoy the splendid panorama of the city and see the spectacular sunsets.

I remember as a highlight my first walk on the wall. It was the scale that was so surprising. Broad as a modern highway, perfectly level, paved and straight into what seemed the far distance, it was a wonderful unexpected perspective stretching before me and deepened my admiration for the men who had planned and built a great civilization all those hundreds of years ago.

Then my eye caught something curious. Some way ahead, on a small higher terrace above the wall top, I made out a huge bronze sphere. When we got nearer I saw other old fantastic looking astronomical instruments. Could they be relics of early Chinese astronomy? None of our party knew. But later I learned that the Chinese had indeed worked out an astronomical system of their own. They believed that the Earth was the centre of the Universe and that Sun, Moon and stars revolved around it.

In the seventeenth century some Jesuits arrived in Peking with a present from Louis XIV to the Chinese Emperor, K'ang Hsi. The present was a large celestial bronze globe. And it was this globe I had seen, still here on the wall top! Apparently the Chinese took to mathematics and astronomy eagerly and were soon able to predict such things as eclipses accurately. But when the date of the eclipse was due, it was another matter. Arrayed in their ceremonial robes, they assemble around their western toys and frantically beat their gongs to scare away the dragon that was about to swallow the Sun and the Moon!

But the idea that the Earth was the centre of the Universe died hard. Far later Galileo was threatened with torture by Rome for daring to suggest that the Sun was the pivot of our solar system. But when the West followed it up and agreed, the source of scientific thought moved north and Rome lost its place as the oracle of truth.

Further on we came to the huge deserted gatehouse that topped the eastern gate, the HaTaMen. Near to, it was quite forbidding, towering three or more storeys above the wall with its immense overhanging double roof. Many windows lay along its walls and there was a small doorway, open and inviting, at wall level.

On the spur of the moment we thought it would be an adventure to go inside and see what it was like. Now it was evening and there was something eerie about its huge abandoned emptiness. How many years was it since hundreds of Chinese soldiers must have been housed here with orders not to look down on their city and their Emperor! Now there was only this small wooden stairway. It looked as if the treads were covered with velvet, grey and soft under our feet. But it was dust! Thick, soft dust! Those stairs must have been undisturbed for years!

We stopped on the steps, rather awed by the silence and a strange smell that pervaded the gloom of the place. Then, I suppose, to break the spooky nervous feeling, one of us clapped hands! Suddenly we were overwhelmed by a whirling stinking presence: bats! Hundreds of bats had taken wing. They were fluttering all around us, over and under us. It was sudden, alarming, frightening. The air was full of their smell, their beating wings and squeaky cries. Then, just as suddenly, they were gone. They streamed out. We saw their crazy silhouettes through a window. In a moment it was all over, but it was spooky. I never went back to the place again.

⌣⋅⌣

Peking had so excited and overwhelmed me by its variety, novelty and beauty, I had quite forgotten we had come for a purpose—to teach these wonderful people to fly!

But before long the Vickers Compradore told us that a representative of the Chinese Air Force would like to meet us and take us down to see their airport at a place called Nan Yuan, a few miles south of the city.

When we got there, the airfield was a huge desolate nothing, fringed with tumbledown barracks, three wooden sheds, a miscellany of grey roofed single storey huts, all of it meagre, dusty, bare and somehow blasted.

General Ting, in charge of Chinese aviation—he knew as much about flying as a caterpillar—was waiting to meet us there, together with his ADC, a slick, American-educated Chinese, with a voluble flow of imperfect English and a broad Yankee accent. With them were a pair of Chinese interpreters, followed by a file of what we supposed must be the would-be pilots of the future Chinese Air Force.

I had never thought much about what our prospective pupils would be like, but this group of young men, whose long silk coats swept in unbroken line from shoulder to ankle, was certainly not like anything we had expected. Clasped hands hidden in their sleeves, they bowed, timid and smiling, the little red buttons in the centre of their black skull caps, nodding brightly at us. They were introduced—Mr Ma, Mr Lu, Mr Ch'ing, Mr Chen, each proffering a delicate hand which emerged magically from the long sleeves and then, clasping the other, disappeared again.

'They are greatly honoured to meet their illustrious teachers and hope, with your help, to learn many things.'

Remembering my early days, how my instructor was a sort of god to me, I smiled reassuringly at them, they were so eager and so young—but those long robes looked frail and somehow out of place. Teaching them to fly would be incongruous—like teaching a mouse to manage a Mosquito.

We trooped out to inspect their machines. I don't know what comment they expected, but faced with them, we burst out laughing. They were pre-war Caudrons, with three-cylinder Anzani engines, 1912 vintage, 'real antiques, made by the ancient Greeks'. The fabric, rotten and yellow with age, hung from the wings, the bracing wires were red with rust, the tyres on the wheels had been replaced with pieces of strong rope.

'Perhaps we would like to give them a flying exhibition?' We politely but firmly refused—the only time, I think I have refused to take a machine into the air. We said the type was not familiar to us. But soon the new machines would be here and we would teach them everything. The new machines! Their eyes gleamed for a moment through their impassivity—ah, yes! The new machines!

They conducted us back to an empty room where they regaled us, western style, with sweet champagne and dry biscuits. It was all they could do. Somehow I was sorry for them. We came from another world and they had no idea whatever what they were in for.

Then, with much bowing and expressions of mutual esteem, we got back into our Firewagon and drove back towards the city.

Driving back I saw for the first time how Peking stands alone on a flat plain, backed by the Western Hills, which lie to the north and west of the city. Running north from the airfield, the South Wall with its big front door, the Ch'ien Men gate, lay before us.

Our road, had it been as originally planned, would have run due north to this gate, on through other walls and gates, right through the centre of the Forbidden City and the Room of Supreme Harmony, bisecting the very body of the Son of Heaven, as he sat on his Throne at the Centre of the World!

It was the inspired belief in a divine revelation of a direction in life. This they had made mathematically practical to stand as the root of their religion which made China believe she was the undisputed ruler of the world.

On either side of our road stretched the plain, flat and fertile, everywhere cultivated with rice, maize, gowliang, and liberally manured with human excrement—there is no drainage system: everything is carried out of the city in wheelbarrows. But there is plenty of fresh water. Wherever you dig, at a depth of ten to fifteen feet, there seems to be water, as if the whole plain were only a skin over an immense underground lake. This water is raised by primitive wheels or endless chains of buckets, worked by little rotating donkeys, blindfolded to stop them going giddy, or else by human treadmills.

Along the roadside grovelling in the dust, were innumerable beggars, displaying fearful self-inflicted sores, arms paralysed from holding them for years above their heads, atrophied legs, monstrous goitres, all bobbing and begging piteously (but professionally—there is a union) for coppers from the rich who sometimes passed by in rickshaws on the way to a temple where they would burn joss for easy childbirth.

But, back that day, on the road from the airport, we paused at the outer gate to be shown some deep banks around a pool. These were primitive and age-old refrigerators in which winter ice from the pool is broken up and stored. It remains frozen all through the spring to be sold to the thirsty in the piping summer months. For the climate is one of extremes; a bitter winter, a sudden short-lived spring, great heat with stormy tropical rain and a languid and exquisite autumn. Except during the rains, it is dry and brittle, a crystalline procession of perfect days, unbroken save for dust-storms—opaque as old time London fogs and as yellow, swirling maelstroms that penetrate everywhere—and the occasional and how welcome high overcast day.

Once within the gate begins that long processional way running between the great Temples of Heaven and Agriculture which flank it right and left, leading upward towards the city gates proper. Laid by Ch'ien Lung in white marble it is in sad disrepair, one block missing meaning a foot-deep pot-hole, so our Firewagon turns along beside it over the hard mud, raising a long plume of dust.

Now we are at the outskirts of the 'Chinese' city, which clusters close under the main walls. The road is wide. At either side stretch dusty wastes as wide as it again. Here pass camel trains with baskets of coal, dirty dignified processions, tied nose to tail; shaggy jaded mules, six to a team, dragging heavy loads, perhaps come down a thousand miles from the deserts of the north: Peking carts with blue cotton hoods and well groomed beasts; shiny broughams with trotting Mongol ponies, very mettlesome and fine; barrows piled with fruits or vegetables, the huge central wheel groaning and the sweating coolie straining his shoulders to balance the heavy pannier loads; cars, sedan chairs, bicycles, a multitude of rickshaws, and all the drivers, bearers, runners shouting, greeting abusing each other, while, weaving in about between them, the watermen fling great ladlefuls of the cool stuff underfoot to lay the choking dust.

From the shops, which flank it all comes the sound of hammering: coppersmiths at work on bowls and saucepans, ironmongers, blacksmiths and silversmiths. Tea houses, shoeshops, food shops, shops for clothes, umbrellas, harness, lanterns, grain, joss, coffins, jewellery, gramophones or jade.

᪥

It was three hundred years ago that the Emperor K'ang Ksi founded the Imperial Factories and brought practised craftsmen from all over China to Peking to work in them. Their range was remarkable. From metal work to maps, from glass to cloisonné, from gilding to lanterns, artificial flowers, optical instruments, jewellery, ivory carving, clocks and lacquer. They were all up to and even beyond the level of work at their time.

The remnants of this pioneering remain today in many trades which have settled together in Furniture St., Lantern St., Kingfisher Feather St.. They work out of small shops, with wooden shutters and open fronts. All display a trademark, sign or streamer, a long blue hanging pennant with white characters upon it.

So the whole vista, swirling with traffic, its banks fluttering with swaying flags, is like a torrent, gushing out under the ornamental *p'ai-lous* and dominated beyond by the great mass of the Ch'ien Men gate.

We had reached the outskirts of the 'Chinese' city and my eye was attracted at once to what looked like a huge cardboard box which stood high above the other shops and hovels along the roadside.

When I pointed, the Interpreter who was with us in the car, said 'Chinese Theatre!' and laughed 'There sing, dance. Many people.' It looked like the covering you sometimes see put up to hide a building under construction. But the covering here was so incredibly tatty and abandoned looking, I couldn't imagine how it could be a theatre.

It wasn't till some months later, during the summer, that I was taken one evening with some Chinese friends to that same theatre to meet the actor who was the most popular 'star' in the play running in Peking at that time, Mei Lun Fang. It was really fantastic. The whole place was a huge structure of matting and bamboo, seating thousands of people in the 'stalls', at ground level, with an upper tier of 'boxes' surrounding them. It was, I remember thinking at the time, a fantastic fire hazard!

The first impression on entering was a cheerful buzz of general audience conversation, quite ignoring a 'play' that was going on at the same time on the huge, 'musical comedy' sized stage which filled one 'end' of this box. There seemed to be no seats anywhere, the 'public', on the ground floor, was all confined in what looked like small pens where they were happily squatting on the ground, eating a meal, feeding their children, talking to each other and their neighbours and generally enjoying themselves.

Every now and then at, I suppose, some point in the action of the play, the whole audience combined in a round of applause and then returned to their private pleasures while the play continued.

Through this warm sweaty atmosphere we pushed our way up some stairs to our box next to the stage. It was just another empty box with planks on the floor and a low wall to look out over. Some rough stools had been provided for 'foreigners' to sit on. Looking down on an audience is always an interesting experience, but this really was something.

Lots of people were lying fast asleep, others were sucking pink jelly sweets or spitting out sunflower seeds or breastfeeding their young and always talking, talking, talking. From time to time a man in one of these pens would stand up and wave his hand. This was to say he wanted a scalding towel to cool himself! And, sure enough, right across from the other side of the auditorium, a cry would precede the throwing of such a towel high up, over the heads of all the spectators, to land pat in his lap. It was such an astonishing feat of marksmanship, I found it much better than the play. But why do scalding towels cool you in boiling hot weather? Mystery!

The whole atmosphere was easy, happy and quite unhurried. Plays, I was told, went on for days, and nobody could explain to me what they were about! But that didn't matter. The general spectacle was quite enough and when, after a special spatter of cymbals and drums, obviously pointed at us, the 'star' appeared in our box, it really did top the evening.

We had seen the spectacle of this beautiful girl, sumptuously dressed, twirling a long white wand and executing a series of steps, half dance, half ritual, send the audience into a whirl of applause, but when she was there, with us, in close up, it was quite different. She had an impressive presence, was magnificently dressed in silk and jewels and spoke quietly and seriously. Obviously the Chinese with us looked on her as somebody almost supernatural.

She extended her hand from her sleeve towards me and I felt the grip of a man's rough handshake! I didn't know what to say, still half unable to believe that this dream of beauty—for she really did convey a magical glittering presence—was only a made-up, middle aged man. So I muttered some platitude of thanks, bowed and smiled, feeling quite unequal to the occasion, as indeed I was.

But now, after many years, I still retain a lively memory of the scene, the heat, the noise and smell of the crowded house, the sense of occasion, of being an outsider, allowed, for a moment, to get the feel of being a guest of something absolutely Chinese at the heart of quite another way of exciting vigorous life.

*T*HE COMPRADORE WISHED TO ENTERTAIN us to Chinese Chow. Would we care to visit the Peony Temple and take tiffin with him there? It was one of Peking's glorious spring days. Everything was coming into flower and we accepted gladly.

'If you are wise' said a friend, 'you will take some envelopes with you.'

'Envelopes! What on earth for?'

'To put the food into.'

'But I like Chinese food.'

'I dare say; but take some envelopes, all the same.'

The temple was outside the city and, like all Chinese temples, restful, quiet and unassuming. But it was springtime and courtyard beds were full of peonies, scarlet and white, just breaking into bloom. We were entranced. It was so typical of the Chinese to dedicate a temple to the growing of a favourite flower. We wandered round admiring till we were called to table.

Our host sat on the south side. Opposite him, on the north, sat the chief guest, and the less important graded round to west and east, while the insignificants sat immediately on his left or right hand. The compass again, not only for a city but for the etiquette of a banquet.

Then the food appeared. It had, of course, been ordered in advance and sent out to the temple, complete with cooks, coolies and boys. Even in the city you would never expect to enter an eating house and sit down to a meal. Food was a serious matter, to be pondered over. You informed the place that you were considering honouring them with your custom. They sent a headman to talk to you about it some days before. You discussed the place, the guests, the dishes in season. There would be regulation numbers, eight, twelve or more. '*A la carte*' did not exist. It was real *table d'hôte* and the host gave himself infinite pains to be sure you would like his table. Then there were the wines, the date, the time, the price per head. It was a long and delicate business, requiring real aesthetic sense: a meal should be a poem.

Of all this we were informed as we were offered a variety of unexpected but delicious hors d'oeuvres. When such a lot of trouble had been taken on our account, we certainly could not be discourteous. Besides the dishes were good. We did justice to them.

But these were nothing, mere appetizers; the meal had not yet begun. Already more than half replete, we began to look at the big bowls askance. They were set down centrally on the table. The host with his own chopsticks helped the guests he wished to honour, the rest helped themselves, dipping their private chopsticks into the public dish.

It was impossible to refuse the host's proffered morsels, saying 'No!' was mere politeness, a formula no one dreamed of taking seriously. Dish after dish! All the usual delicacies were brought out and many that I can't now remember. It seemed interminable. It was a sign of appreciation to make noises as you ate, to suck up your soup like a walrus, say ah! and belch loud and long to the table at large.

It was equally proper to rise without leave, walk up and down, talking and chewing sunflower seeds from a side table. This was an interval, helped to settle the food and whetted the appetite for the next dish. At last after some eighteen dishes, the sweets! Well, it hadn't been so bad after all. We hadn't had to use the envelopes.

Premature relief, for our host explained that in a Chinese meal the sweets come in the centre, a custom left over from the days when meals were really meals, when banquets lasted all day long and guests ate sweet in the warm part of the day. We smile wanly, fingering the envelopes in our pockets.

For you could not refuse, could not leave things in your bowl, yet when you cleared it surreptitiously into a paper in your lap, came the immediate response: 'Ah! You like this dish! Come a little more! Come! This is the last dish. (It was the twenty sixth.) Please!'

At last it was over. We were groaning, bursting, speechless. And then the rice appeared! Great steaming lacquered bowls of rice. A helping as big as a Christmas pudding was placed before us. This was not the meal. This was just a chaser to fill up any vacant crevices. 'Eat a little! Please! It is healthy to end a meal so!' And the good man laughed and continued to discuss his piles, a subject he seemed to find of absorbing interest.

Among the Chinese to have a *da doudza*—a big stomach—is a sign of wealth and well being. Perhaps we should grow accustomed to it, for there was little sustaining in the food. After three or four hours we found we were ravenous again!

At last we got away with profuse expressions of delight and gratitude, climbed gingerly into our cars because of the pockets bursting with their envelopes and lay back, exhausted. Though there was no wind the peonies seemed to sway in the courtyard.

But now looking back on that smiling far away day of my youth, I am filled with an extraordinary nostalgia. The setting, the warmth in the old Temple, the shadows, the flowers that welcomed us as their guests, the etiquette of our host, the care he had given to the robes in which he would preside over the meal, the silent attentive servants, the formal words of welcome, the geniality, the generosity, all this was showing us what China was, what she had stood for down the ages, courtesy, etiquette, love of company, love of giving and in the guests the pleasure of receiving. I retain a certain humility at being honoured to have taken part in such a feast. Now, in the evening of old age, the scent of that summer day melts into enchantment. Did I really sit at that table? Was I privileged to taste, even as an uncouth foreigner, such a ballet of another time, another way of life.

⌣∴∾

I slept little. In the night I would hear the tap-tap-tap of bamboos, the watchman going his rounds. His idea was not to catch the thieves, but to warn them he was coming. Then with the first light, the herons would rise from the yews in the Palace courtyards and sail, like grey majestic ghosts, down to their feeding grounds in the reed lakes beyond the walls.

Soon the first street vendors would begin their calls. I heard the water carriers pass, the wheels of their barrows creaked when they were laden, empty they made no sound. To his spokes the coal-seller fastened little bells, so that his wheel passed with a jingling that brought people to their doors. The knife-grinder used a shrill trumpet to announce himself, the fruitseller clanged two brass cups, the barber a sort of tuning fork which plucked, made a long dying note sound. All these I heard below, mingled with calls and cries and camel bells; the confused mutter of the waking city, an indistinct persistent murmur like sea-sounds from a shell.

The streets were busy from dawn. There was a lot of day-to-day business done at the door. The shoemaker set down his last at any customer's steps, a broken plate could be rivetted, your hair or your toes cut, you could buy your meat or your 'sweet water' from a passing wheelbarrow. You threw out your rubbish (and urine) into the street, but not your excrement, that was sold to be wheelbarrowed off to the nearest vegetable farmer's plot. You shopped and lived at your front door. Life came to you, you didn't go to it. In spite of the filthy, smelly streets (I was told) the city was healthy. It was dry and hot and that seemed to keep the dreaded epidemics away.

Sometimes military bands would pass, playing western instruments with ghastly eastern harmony, a blatant comical braying that would have made Hindemith blush for his orthodoxy. The matting and bamboo in the market were blazing, but all the same, there was order and ceremony to be observed. True, the hand pumps could not throw the water twelve feet high; true, by the time they got there even London's Fire Brigade would have been put to it to dowse the roaring mass, but what of that? Their water would squirt finely till it was exhausted, the fire would then be left to burn itself out and the gallant brigade would return, something attempted, nothing done, the band playing louder than ever.

On propitious days there were funerals. A long procession lined each side of the road, while the traffic passed, unheeding between it. Innumerable mourners and musicians hired for the occasion, blew sobbing notes from long golden horns; then the hearse, a huge ponderous catafalque, draped and hooded with crimson, embroidered with blue and gold, borne slowly on the shoulders of a hundred coolies, with one ahead, tapping two sticks to mark the time. Death was important—and very expensive. A man's place in life was shown in the pomp of his death.

The chief mourner followed the hearse, dressed all in white, sitting on the shaft of a Peking cart, head in hand, a pensive attitude of ceremonial grief. Behind him came other mourners, walking, white robed, spitting thoughtfully from time to time; after these effigies of wives, houses, furniture, motorcars—all in paper to be burned—relic of the days when a man's wives and goods were really destroyed with him.

Another day would come the quicker rattle of the executioner's cart, the victim strapped, standing in it naked to the waist and the soldier's ponies trotting cheerfully behind. After the madness of the summer wars, rebels were executed sometimes

48

twenty at a time, beyond the walls. They didn't seem to mind. When they were made to kneel in a row, hands tied behind their backs, they watched those who went before and laughed as their heads rolled off, struck with the great two-handed sword.

Whether it was a funeral or a wedding. I could see little difference in the pomp of the processions. In the wedding little urchins carried gifts in glass-topped cases, showing them through the streets. Crimson tubular umbrellas preceding the bride in her gay, hooded, lacquered showcase, going secret to meet her unknown husband: the bridegroom's family waiting to receive her and, if all was well, displaying the next morning at the street door, on white silk, the scarlet evidence of her virginity. (But wise women, it was said, knew tricks with pigeon's blood to counterfeit such things.)

At last the sun would set behind the Western Hills. Night would come down. Lights would glow through paper windows. The city quieted. At half past nine the great gates were swung to. Now none might enter till the morning.

*I*T WAS ONE DAY, RETURNING FROM the airfield, that we received
a wonderful piece of news, wonderful for us anyway.
Contractual difficulties had arisen between Vickers Ltd and the
Chinese Government, holding up the whole deal! Delivery of
the aeroplanes was postponed till the autumn. Meanwhile we
were to remain here and hang on. This was unbelievable news!
To be stranded in the wonderland of Peking for 6 months on a
good salary with nothing to do but enjoy ourselves! This was
Luck, with a capital l!

Here was a chance really to get to know the city in all its
variety and beauty, to explore the temples, visit the Summer
Palace, the Great Wall and find those hidden places in the
Western Hills I had heard spoken of! I could collect some
antiques, try to learn some Mandarin Chinese, and even,
marvellous idea, live in a Chinese house of my own! This was so
unexpected and so exciting, I got absolutely hooked on it!

I think this was because a Chinese house is quite different
from anything built in the West. To start with it is all on the
ground floor, all laid out in courtyards and all, like a Chinese
city, planned by compass, its doorway on the south. Its
courtyards open one out of another, first one for the servants
and kitchens, then another for dependents or relations, then the
living quarters themselves, and behind these the sleeping
quarters, the chief wife's pavilions, the place for concubines.

The beauty and complexity of the courts varies with the size
of the house and the wealth of the owner. Each court is flanked
on all four sides by low grey-roofed pavilions into which the

light comes through patterned shutters, backed with rice paper. In wealthy houses each court is decorated differently with lily pool, ornamental bridge, flowering shrub or odd-shaped rock. All, in a lovely house, stand under the shadow of great trees. Passing along the narrow hutungs, under blank walls, you would never guess what beauties lay behind the tall red lacquer doors. It is all mysterious, very secret, a perfect plan for privacy.

All this also sharpened my love of beauty, my feeling for quality and taste. To live in Peking in those days was to be struck just by the colour and variety of everyday life. I surfaced every morning with all the gusto and appetite of my twenty-two years. Peking gave me a love of China and things Chinese that has lasted all my life and though almost all I loved has been lost during the later suicidal years, I believe the innate qualities of life the Chinese knew and valued will resurface and be their inspiration in years to come.

My little house in Peking was the first home of my own. I didn't plan it or build it as I did others that followed, but it gave me all my first experiences of creating something out of nothing and enjoying the secret pleasures of pride and ownership.

I don't remember how I found it. Somebody must have found it for me. It was in the maze of lanes that ran east of the HaTaMen, the big highway that carried the traffic on that side of the city. It was small and neat, with three courtyards, a place for the servants by the door, a big courtyard—with a cherry tree actually in flower!—a big north living room, two bedrooms, one on the west and the other on the east wall.

The sanitary and washing arrangements were primitive. Water would be brought by the wheelbarrow water boy and all the waste disappeared with a call from the dustbin barrow boy. My boy, the coolie, the cook and the motorman (for I had bought a second hand car) all lived together in one room by the front door. It had a raised platform at one end, the common bed, under which, in winter, a fire could be lit.

Now, having got the house the next thing to do was to furnish it. And that faced me with the Great Problem—language!

ᴗ∵ᴖ

Chinese is a language of extreme difficulty. To start with, in the written language, there are no letters, no alphabet. The hieroglyphs, or 'characters', run right to left—'backwards'—or up and down. And they are 'written' with a brush! Even scholars take years to master their own language.

The spoken word varies all over China. To such an extent does it differ that when my friend's boy from Shanghai wished to talk to my boy in Peking, they had to write down what they wished to say in pidgin English!

The Mandarin (official) language has four tones or intonations. The same sound such as, for example, *ka* can mean mosquito, smoke, a pair of spectacles or blue, according to the tone, the intonation, in which you pronounce it. Once, entertaining Chinese to dinner, I thought to air my Chinese by asking my boy to bring in another chair, '*Nah eedze li*'. But I had said '*eedza*' in the wrong tone and the boy appeared a moment later with a cake of soap!

And, of course, the vocabulary is vast. The average westerner employs, I believe, about ten thousand words. The Bible has a wider range and Shakespeare uses about twenty-five thousand. An educated Chinese may go up to forty thousand and as all the characters can be hyphenated or doubled, the possibilities are endless.

At the other end of the scale, the coolie gets along with two to three hundred words. Some of these three hundred I had managed to acquire. At any rate I knew enough to find my way about the city and price or buy what I wanted. So furnishing became a daily adventure.

I remember bargaining over blackwood tables and chairs, watching the men polishing them by holding a shovel of redhot charcoal over the wood and applying the wax underneath so that it went in hot. Shovel and hand moved back and forth over the surface till it shone like a mirror and would not mark as our 'french' polish will. Years later, back in London, when I dusted these chairs, still with me, they shone as brightly as on the day I bought them.

I haggled over hangings and cooking pots, over rugs, divans and lanterns. I spent hours at the Imperial Goldfish Ponds selecting exquisite banner tails. The men who sold them told me how in the winter the water—and the fish—froze solid! In the spring when the ice melted these beauties sailed out alive, none the worse for months in their crystal coffins.

I visited temple market fairs, night markets, flea markets, thieves' markets, picking up crockery, porcelain, pictures, curios and despising much I would gratefully own today. It was not only the pleasure of buying and bargaining, it was the teeming life about the stalls that never ceased to fascinate and charm.

Tall Manchu women in their gorgeous embroidered robes, strolling in groups, with their flawless enamelled make up, heavily white powdered and rouged (to show the white origin they claim), their high black headdresses and their sandals with heels in the middle beneath their insteps, making them walk with stiff stately grace. I only once saw an old-style Manchu man, or Mandarin, as he was called, in his sable robe, belted with jade and a golden clasp, from which hung spectacles, ivory chopsticks and a handsome jewelled watch. He was a relic of the past, but a striking picture of the lifestyle such dignitaries retain—'when he went from the Palace in his green sedan chair or in his closed Peking cart with a handsome mule caparisoned in red, surrounded by outriders shrieking to clear the way for their master. Simple folk looked on him with respect and awe; the patchwork of idlers pressing themselves against the walls as the procession went by. This was an event in their workday lives, a sort of Lord Mayor's Show to be excited and proud of.'

But side by side with the wealthy were the Mongols down from the north, thoughtfully chewing a sugared necklace of red crab-apples as they bargained; children with their four still plaits, like dolls, playing around the toy stalls; old men with long thin drooping moustaches, fanning themselves, reflective over the scent of a flower; sober peasants in stolid black or gay teahouse girls in their short tunics and bright trousers. All life was there, from satin to cotton, from childhood to dotage and it was all happy and genial. By the time I had finished I knew every quarter in the city and had shopkeeping friends in every street.

Meanwhile back at the house, the plasterers were touching up the walls, painting the windows and repapering the paper ceilings. The vine and the wisteria had been dug out from their hard winter and a jobbing carpenter was making good the shutters. He was a strange man that carpenter, a symbol of the age long traditions of China where things were still done as they had been a thousand years ago.

I had bought a 'crackled ice' screen. The crackled ice design is, I believe, one of the oldest and most poetic of Chinese designs. You may see it on ginger jars, on porcelain, on embroidery, on shutters and windows. Some artist must have seen a lake thawing in the spring and the ice cracking and the almond blossom falling on it. Out of that he created a design: a background of irregular pentagons and hexagons with carved, engraved or painted blossoms at the joints. My screen had four such patterns, each different, all badly broken, one with a big hole in the centre and each with several pieces missing. I spent some time examining the design, trying to find some general formula which would keep it in balance while allowing it to vary in detail; but in spite of measuring angles and the length of the 'cracks', I could find no rule. It seemed a real improvisation.

I asked my boy if we should not get a cabinet maker to repair it. No, he said, this man would do it. So I watched. The repairs were swiftly done without hesitation or measurement. Each piece seemed to fall naturally into place and when it was complete I could not tell the new from the old. The four patterns were all perfect. To what jobbing carpenter in the UK, I thought, would you entrust some damaged Chippendale?

At last I left the wonderful look-out from my hotel window and stood, one late autumn evening, surveying my own courtyard. It was quite a moment for me. The boy, the cook, the coolie, the motorman and the rickshaw runner were all below by the door settling in, chattering before they rolled up onto the *kang*, the stone dais of a bed. Behind them light glowed through paper windows. Within were all the things I had collected with such zest and care. I was a very proud and contented householder at twenty-two.

*I*T IS SAID THAT THE STATE of any country can be judged by
the extent to which it is guided and governed by its religion.
China is an empire of largely self-governing states or provinces,
all owing, until recently, a nominal homage to the northern
government of Peking. My brief visit was to Peking, in northern
China and everything I saw or experienced refers to the capital
city and the country round about.

I cannot explain why the first impression of Peking was, to
me, 'flavoured' with the sense of it being a city of temples.
Perhaps it was my first sight of the overwhelming beauty and
majesty of the Forbidden City, which, though it was essentially
a Royal Palace, radiated a sense of awe and worship for the
Emperor of China. Worship is a sort of reverence of some
superhuman being or spirit and given to persons whose
position or bearing is thought to give them superiority over their
fellow men and worthy to receive it.

This flavour of religion being an accepted part of daily life
was certainly confirmed when I began to read up guidebooks
about the city. I found there were almost 2,000 temples in
Peking! Over a thousand of these were places of worship of
different religious faiths and over two thousand priests,
Buddhist, Taoist, Lama, Moslem, and Christian looked after
them.

But these statistics were easily and completely absorbed by
the geniality and good humour of the people. Down the ages
they had repeatedly received new beliefs and new faiths and
accepted them with tolerance as an added wealth to their daily

life. All could believe what they like, provided it did not lead to public disorder.

Looking back on those days I retain an overall sense of peace and quietness of heart. There was no hurry. Time was not the whip of life. People may say this had nothing to do with religion, but I feel certain that a basic faith in 'something', quite natural and unobtrusive, was the ground of it all. People were not governed, they governed themselves.

I remember how strong I felt all this when, for the first time, I walked through the main entrance into the first courtyard of the Forbidden City. All that I had looked down on from my hotel window seemed quite different at ground level. I got quite another sense of scale.

The place looked huge. The courtyard stretched away like a waste land of flagstones and white marble. It was absolutely empty, absolutely silent. Through it meandered a small stream under five small white marble bridges and ahead, raised on two terraces, stood the entrance to the Great Courtyard of the Throne Room of the Emperor.

Entering this Royal Courtyard was to be met by an impact of such dignity, nobility and beauty that all description belittles it. Twice as large as the forecourt I had come through, there was nothing on its far side but one great lonely room, the Throne Room, the heart of the Forbidden City. It stood on three wide terraces, all edged with white marble balustrades consisting of hundreds of serpentine columns topped by a lintel. This decorative feature braided the edges of all the terraces in the courtyard.

The Throne Room itself stood on a wide marble terrace which itself stood on three lower terraces and was reached by two broad flights of steps rising either side of the central 'Spirit Way', a rising slope of carved white marble panels on which the unseen presences could approach the Throne unimpeded by the feet of mortal men. The effect of such a glitter of white stone against a blue sky was so dazzling that the Throne Room itself seemed to be floating weightless on a cloud.

It took time for my eyes to adjust to the dim light within, as I stepped through one of the tall open doorways. When I began to be able to focus and look around me, I saw that I was standing, literally, in a Room! A huge empty Room of slightly scented age, supported by rows of great columns which held a complex arrangement of beams and rafters, all decorated with designs in deep red, green and snatches of bright yellow. All this, seen above in the dim light gave only a blurred impression of the beauty and technical complexity of these wonderful Chinese roofs, all put together without nail or bolt and standing for centuries on columns holding up the immense load of heavy ornamental tiles.

These wooden columns were fashioned from the largest tree trunks to be found in China—now to be found no more. So when, more recently, there was a threat to the Temple of Heaven an urgent appeal was made to America. She alone could produce and send over the gigantic Oregon columns necessary to repair its roof.

Standing there in the dim light that filtered through the paper windows of this one-time Centre of the Past, its empty loneliness seemed a full stop to all past glories. Yet, such is the power of imagination, it is possible for those who have been close to it, to bring it back.

It is midnight. The Ch'ien men—the main gate that leads to the Chinese City is opened by the Guard. The wailing creak of wooden hubs mingles with the rumble of wheels and the clatter of the hooves of the mules on the stone pavement as a string of carts comes through. Down frozen streets this is a procession of minor courtiers slowly moving to an audience with the Emperor.

They reach the East and West Gates, sitting tailor-fashion in their furlined robes, crosslegged in their springless carts and get down still-legged to make their way to the courtyard before the

T'Ai Ho Tien. There they take their places according to their rank, marked by a small bronze triangle in the shape of a mountain. There is no talking. A weird sort of tension fills the air, as always in court ceremonies where nobody knows what will happen and men stare into each other's eyes asking questions which perhaps they do not know they ask. In the courtyard below tribute elephants stand in the four corners like statues and gilded bronze cisterns filled with oil blaze like cauldrons of fire.

Since the comings and goings of the Sovereign are subject to the stars, the courtiers wait patiently, shivering in their sable robes, for the hour fixed by the Board of Astronomy when the Emperor will appear. Just as dawn breaks a courtier announces that the Imperial Procession is almost about to start and all present fall on their knees.

Far away in those inner courts the Imperial cortege has gathered. Slowly it winds its way past the lesser throne halls and through the Ch'ien Ching Men past the Ch'ien Ching Kung. Excitement spreads through the crowds of courtiers as the drums announce the Herald: 'He comes! He comes! The Lord of Ten Thousand Years!' One last dividing wall and the magnificent pageant is in sight; the brilliant banners, the heavy bodyguards, the attendant Princes and Ministers and finally the Ruler of the World in his yellow satin-draped chair with its gilded dragons.

Then immediately all fall to their knees and bow their foreheads nine times to the ground, greeting their Sovereign with that hoarse shout—a cheer, but not a cheer: 'Ten thousand years! Ten thousand years!'

The golden chair is carried up the high steps to the 'Dragon Pavement'. The Emperor alights. He enters the Hall, whose panelled ceiling with its five-clawed dragons is the emblem of imperial power and masculine strength. An awed silence follows him as he walks past the crimson and gold supporting pillars glowing soberly in the lantern light to mount the platform to the Dragon Throne and seats himself in the prescribed attitude, his hands upon his knees, his eyes downcast. Then the Princes and dignitaries come forward, prostrate themselves to offer New Years Greetings...

(Juliet Bredon, *Peking*)

Whoever has seen such a ghostly ceremony in the pale dawn can never return to these noble palaces without feeling the pulse of an ancient civilization which throbbed as mightily in the eighteenth century as in that remote past of which they are but a modern record. In these vast halls there is something more than architectural splendour, a sort of magical echo of another age, a superb pageant of a time with different needs, different hopes and a destiny that believed in itself, its future and a fortunate life to come.

*I*T COMES NATURALLY TO FOLLOW my memories of the Forbidden City, perhaps the most famous and magnificent palace ever made for a ruler of men to the monuments these same rulers made to glorify the Being they believed to be all powerful yet invincible, dwelling in palaces 'not made with hands.'

There must have been some far off time when human beings discovered themselves, when they recognized they were what they called 'alive' and could create life, that they could rejoice in living and loving, but that they were, alas, mortal, their bodies would fail or be broken and that life, whatever it was, would withdrew itself from them and they would die.

This was the time when they first saw themselves and their place in the natural world about them. Later they began to recognize they were also part of a world that was not as they were: the sea did not give birth to renew itself, nor did the air bear children. Their life had needs of a higher order, which remained (and still remains) a mystery to them.

Above all stood the Sun, the Majestic Creator of all life, whose commands had to be obeyed and worshipped. This everpresent divinity also remained a mystery for although its commands and laws were didactic, absolute, it seemed to them to be, as it were, the mouthpiece or messenger of some yet greater Presence beyond itself.

So, after many centuries of discussion and meditation, being unable to reach any firm understanding, these ancients concluded that the 'something' they called God was a Divine

Mystery, all seeing, all knowing, which compelled them to worship Him. To Him they must dedicate their lives as servants to this Unknown God.

It also appeared to them that certain places on the surface of the earth were more suitable than others to offer up this worship and, as if to confirm their faith, a revelation was made to one of them. Casually swinging a stone on the end of a long stalk of grass, he noticed that it always came to rest facing in the same direction. Passing the time idly playing with this curiosity, he called it to the attention of others, serious thinking men.

What supernatural power caused certain sorts of stone always to settle pointed towards the same goal with such determined, unwavering precision? Overcome with awe, after long and deep deliberation the wise men decided this was a sacred confirmation of a Source calling them towards the Throne of their unknown God. Accordingly it was decreed that henceforth all their lives, their cities, temples, palaces, streets and houses should point the way to the source of this God it had been given to them to follow.

The discovery of this invisible direction finder, later known as the compass, became the root of all navigation. It had its original birthplace in one of the three, four or fives cities built on the same sacred site on which Peking, the original capital city of China, was born. Here the Perfect Emperors offered their sacrifices more than 4,000 years ago.

All this great reservoir of holiness and sacred dedication was swept aside forgotten in the turmoil when the last Emperor abdicated and China was decreed a Republic in 1912. Only these sacred precincts of old days remained.

But, living as a visitor in the city, I retain a very deep and powerful sense of China having its own special atmosphere, very quiet and dignified, which seemed somehow to absorb these intruders and make them part of its own culture.

I remember very well the morning I went to visit the Temple

and Altar of Heaven. I entered the 'park', a large (700 acre) open, empty grass slope surrounded by hedges of yew. There near the head of it, stood the Temple, alone, on its three superb white marble terraces. But slowly, as I gazed and gazed at it, I was overcome by a feeling of sadness. This unique, glorious circular shrine, with its dark blue triple roofs, a famous beauty—almost the 'trademark' of China—did not feel 'right'. Something was wrong. What had happened?

The perfection of the Temple of Heaven lies in the subtlety of its proportions. Its solid almost squat appearance from below looks slim from a distance. Its quiet isolation from the hubbub of the city, its presence, its beauty and the gorgeous wealth of its deep blue roofs (found on no other building in China) make it unforgettable, unique. The Temple is an architectural showpiece, a symbol of spiritual belief as important to China as the Pyramids to Egypt or Stonehenge to England.

Springing up from its three tiers of white terraces, with their carved balustrades the Temple of Heaven rises ninety-nine feet into the air. It is simply a shrine supported by huge wooden columns. These take the weight of the roofs, one above the other. But the complexity and beauty of the Temple is almost impossible to describe. There are three roofs, one above the other, but the two lower roofs are really more like veranda shades over the windows below them. Only the top circular roof grows to a triumphant apex and is surmounted by a large gold knob.

In 1889 the Temple was struck by lightning and burned to the ground—a disaster explained by the intrusion of a presumptuous centipede which dared to climb up to the topmost golden dome. To rebuild it was the only way to appease the wrath of God at such flagrant disrespect.

With help from America, Oregon pine for the four main columns was procured. These, shaped and lacquered, supported the great roof and twelve smaller ones the two lighter roofs below. Dragons and phoenixes returned to inhabit the cross beams with their crimson and gold. The windows, open wooden traceries backed with white paper and doors with brass hinges and gilded bosses, all this was rebuilt back to its former glory to become a venerated antique, a tribute to a glorious past.

But now all the Sacred was gone and only the shell of the Temple remained, abandoned, neglected, forgotten. I was terribly disappointed. How could such a sacred place be so forgotten? Had all it stood for become so worthless? I came out thinking it was like some gorgeous costume which had lost its wearer...

From the Temple a broad pathway drops down a gentle slope towards the Altar of Heaven. But before reaching it, there stands the most perfect small shrine in China, called the Imperial World. Under a marvellously simple black tiled roof, it used to hold the Spirit Tablets of the Ch'ing Emperors and later ceremonial objects used in the Altar services.

Almost immediately below it stands the Altar of Heaven. Modelled and remodelled down the centuries, it owes its present magnificence to the Emperor Ch'ien Lung who rebuilt and added to this wonder of white marble.

It stands open to the sky in the centre of a square court surrounded by dull red walls pierced by four white marble archways. Four flights of steps facing the four points of the compass mount to three shining white marble terraces, enclosed by richly carved white marble balustrades. The middle circular stone of the highest platform was considered to be the hub of the Universe. Every detail of the Altar had a deep significance. Conceived with geometrical precision, it was, like the Forbidden City, the combined work of architects, astronomers and doctors of magic.

The Altar of Heaven is the only one dedicated to the worship of the Supreme Deity, the Unknown God, to whom it is a supreme tribute. Multiples of nine appear in the flights of steps of nine each which lead to it, in the total number of balustrades, 360, which surround it and in the 81 pure white marble tiles, out of which the highest terrace is built.

The Altar is without blemish or dedication. Its simplicity and purity are absolute. Its dimensions are sacred and have been carefully planned and laid out. Down the centuries it has been rebuilt and enlarged many times, the last time by the Great Emperor, Ch'ien Lung, as part of his life inspiration to renew the majesty and magnificence of China as ruler of the world.

'The Space upon the Altar is too small,' ran the Ch'ien Lung Edict. 'In planning to substitute a new altar the surface of the three terraces, while still preserving the numerical relation of nine by five, should be enlarged so as to enable those officiating to have more room to move about and show proper reverence. Officers should carefully consider and respect this.'

It was he who enlarged the Altar, rewrote the ritual, designed the precise position of all those taking part in the two great annual ceremonies on the summer and winter solstices. He alone could place his personal shrine on the top terrace, reserved for the dignitaries who chanted the ceremonies, made the offerings and performed the sacred rites. He alone assumed the personal responsibility and right to be the only one worthy to make an offering on behalf of all China, to the Most, Most Sacred Presence of the Unknown God.

When the last Chinese Emperor abdicated in 1912, the first President, Yuan Shih-k'ai, attempted to revive these ceremonies. But the times had gone, the sanctity and devotion no longer existed. The whole park was left empty, almost unvisited and the two unique monuments to man's highest and most sacred aspirations looked forlorn and deserted. Even some 'foreign devils', who shall be nameless, attempted to hold a modern dance on the top terrace of the Altar of Heaven: but this last insult was summarily prevented.

When I stood on this terrace one perfect sunlit morning, only eight years later, and tried to take in the strange sense of emptiness and desertion which seemed to wash in over the Temple and the Altar of Heaven, lying there before me, it seemed to be because, without the sense of worship and love with which they had been created, they were calling, longing, for some renewal of life to give substance and meaning to the love and faith that once inspired them.

∼∴∼

At last, in December, the first machines began to arrive. The mechanics were given quarters at the aerodrome, and the huge crates unpacked. After all this time it was exciting to see an aeroplane again. We had almost forgotten what one looked like. The Avros arrived first. They were quickly erected and tested, and off we crashed, into the air again! It was over a year since I had been up, and I wondered if, in the interim, I had forgotten how to fly, if I had lost the feel of it or should be hesitant or clumsy in the air. The doubt was soon dispelled. It was second nature. I could fly as well as ever.

In parenthesis, it may be of interest to those who have given up flying to wonder whether they could still handle a machine, if the occasion arose. I gave up flying, on leaving China, in 1921, and did not touch a stick again until the summer of 1935—fourteen years later. A friend took me up in a Moth, a machine I had never been in before. It had dual control, and he let me take over. In under a minute I was doing vertical banks with perfect assurance.

Five years later, in 1940, I managed to get back to the RAF, re-learning to fly modern aircraft. I flew all through the World War II, finishing up on Hurricanes and Spitfires. Then, to cap it all off, in 1946, I bought my own aeroplane, a Miles Gemini, and made, my last flight—a 6,000 miles cross country from Reading to Johannesburg!

I was then 47. But at 95, over fifty years later, another friend took me up, as passenger in a Tiger. I felt, perfectly at ease, flew as well as ever, and made a perfect landing! Flying is like riding a bicycle, once you know how, it stays with you.

But back to China.

Soon we had three or four Avros in commission and started instruction. Eight pupils were allotted to me. Before taking them into the air, we gave some lectures on the ground. I tried to explain such mysteries as horizon, bank, engine torque, and so on—all, of course, through my interpreter. Such Western terms were, of course, impossible to translate. Some Chinese equivalent had to be invented. With the aid of a blackboard, I drew diagrams of thrusts, pulls, turning moments; anything which might help to give my pupils some general idea of what made an aeroplane lift, fly straight, turn, or glide. I often wonder how much they understood, for my interpreter, though eager and fluent, must have been as much mystified by it all as they were.

At last we went out and I took them up in turn, trying, on their first lesson, to teach them to fly straight and keep the nose on the horizon. It wasn't a great success. The day was wintry, misty and overcast, so that, as it happened, there was very little horizon to be seen. This flummoxed them completely. As soon as I released the pressure on the rudder, round she went under the torque. As soon as I took my hand off the stick, up went the nose like a lift. Now what was to be done? How to explain? We had no telephones between the cockpits, and even if we had, they would have been no use. Imagine trying to say in Chinese in the air: 'You must use left rudder to counteract the torque. Can't you feel the machine slipping? Can't you feel the wind on the side of your face? That means we are sliding outwards. Put on some left rudder. More! More!'

My pidgin Chinese, good enough to purchase a yard of silk or a pair of candlesticks, couldn't begin to cope with this sort of thing. The only alternative was to switch off and shout some phrase you had learned by heart: Rudder! More rudder! Straight! Keep straight! But if the pupil heard it, he could not tell you so. Besides, in the effort of shouting you might have used the wrong tone and perhaps unknowingly insulted his mother, or inquired about his boots! It was a predicament. The only thing to do, as we soon found out, was to land, explain the difficulty to the interpreter, wait while it was translated, and then start off again. The effect was either nil or else to send the pupil to the opposite extreme: he jammed the rudder hard over and the machine whisked round like a kitten after its own tail.

Besides this there was a curious opacity, a sort of wooden-headed fatalism, a streak of national temperament, that stepped in. One pupil so constituted did what was the equivalent of losing his head, and locked both feet on the rudder bar, pressing them against it so hard that I could not move it and thought for an anxious second that the controls had jammed. I switched off at once and yelled something: 'Take off your feet! Let go!' Useless, it meant nothing. There was the rudder locked central, the machine dithering and slipping, and what could I do about it? Luckily I was stronger in the leg than my pupil, so I got the machine down by main force. But it was unpleasant.

So the instruction went on, day after day, in a temperature about ten degrees below freezing-point; round and round the desolate aerodrome, coming down frozen to explain to a frozen pupil, through a frozen interpreter how, say, to keep his wings level. Couldn't he see he was flying one wing down? Couldn't he see they were not parallel with the horizon? Off went the wretched interpreter in a torrent of angry-sounding Chinese, while the water dripped steadily from his nose. You waited, slapping your numb hands on your thighs. You expected perhaps some reason, some adequate explanation of his idiocy. The conversation stopped. The interpreter turned. 'He is very sorry. Next time he will make great efforts to do better.' It was pathetic. You took off again, let him take over, and down went the wing, just the same as before.

Unquestionably ignorance of the language slowed up instruction; but we soon formed the impression that these Chinese boys were not natural aviators, certainly not for light aeroplanes. They were slow and ham-fisted—strangely, for their hands were so delicate one would have thought that over-lightness would be the fault—and had sluggish reactions. How had they been chosen? We never knew.

This question of the speed of the hand's response to something seen by the eye, the lag between impulse and reflex, is, as every pilot knows, the essence of good judgement; instantaneous reaction is an absolute necessity in putting a light aeroplane down successfully. A split second too early or too late, and you land well above the ground or fly into it. Our pupils, when they went solo, often landed cheerfully twenty feet up. 'He is very sorry. Next time he will make great efforts to do better.' It was a formula. In such circumstances "better" seemed hardly the word.

*A*T THE WINTER SOLSTICE, THE SHORTEST DAY of the year, one of my pupils invited me to his house to witness a firework display. The Chinese were the inventors of gunpowder and, with characteristically civilized instincts, put it to no other use than to make crackers. These crackers in my boyhood were obtainable in London for the 5th of November. Skeins of small scarlet tubes with their fuses plaited together, they could be detached and set off separately or lit as a whole, when they exploded in a series of reports like a young machine gun. Such crackers still have a serious function in China, for they are used in temple ceremonies.

There were quite a company collected to see the display. It was the first time I have been in a truly Chinese house, owned by a Chinese, and at first I was surprised at its simplicity and austerity. (For much of the junk that is sold to tourist and foreigner is specially manufactured for the market and quite alien to the people.) The walls were bare, hung here and there with a few scrolls, four or five large characters, black on a plain white ground. These were poems which appealed, not only on account of the beauty of the thought expressed, but also because of the actual calligraphy. In the West some of us admire fine handwriting; but it is no longer an art in itself. It would not occur to us that the beauty of stanza could be enhanced by the writing of it. Not so in China. The outward clothing of the thought is a supplement to the thought itself: an ornament to beauty.

These scrolls are not permanent decorations as our pictures are. Many are kept in chests, and when the whim takes the owner, he lifts down the one on view and substitutes another. So, in this way, it is possible to clothe the walls with sentiments fitting to the occasion or the season of the year.

At the sides of the room against the walls were pairs of stiff blackwood chairs, a small table between each pair, on which stood an ornament, a vase, or perhaps the diminutive teacups, little bowls holding a tablespoon of golden liquid, a teapot at their side. Sometimes, in spring, growing flowers were to be found on these tables. A flat oblong dish, about an inch deep, of pale green porcelain, would be filled with fine gravel and covered with clear water. A single narcissus bulb, but one carefully selected having three corms, had been placed in the dish. Its roots had grown out, a tenuous white net through the gravel. Its three green shoots had lifted in a lovely pattern of leaf and flower. The size of the dish seemed exactly proportioned to the height of the slender stems, and the whole had a simple unity of perfection.

Standing by such a flower I once observed a very old Chinese. His hair, plaited into a long pigtail, was almost white. He was clad in a white silk robe from ankle to throat, in his hand he held a large golden fan with a poem inscribed upon it. Unaware of my presence, he was standing, wrapped in contemplation of the flower, and very slowly fanning the scent of it towards him.

But this evening the decoration of the room was the people in it. There were many, mostly young. Some were dressed Chinese fashion, some incongruously wore the lounge suits of the West, some combined the two, wearing Homburg hats, horn-rimmed spectacles, and satin robes. The girls, their shiny black hair caught in a single plait, had a fringe in front and wore gay silk coats buttoning at the side, with long tight sleeves and straight-up military-looking neckbands. These coats fitted tightly to their waists. Below were ridiculous and charming little pink trousers, reaching to half-way down the calf, where they finished in a lace fringe. Black stockings and bright pink embroidered shoes completed a captivating effect. But some of the girls, too, affected the Western blouse and skirt, to their detriment, and one successfully outdid all others by displaying a fine pair of whalebone stays, reaching from bust to thigh, tightly laced *outside* her blouse!

The fireworks were to be let off in the courtyard outside. We were called to the window. Coolies staggered in with large flowering trees, standing in their tubs about four feet high. When they came closer I saw they were all made of paper, blossoms, leaves, stalks, trunks complete. At first I did not realize that these were the fireworks. But soon they were lit with tapers. The paper flowers became fiery blossoms. As they subsided their stalks burned, emitting showers of sparks, leaves spurted and hissed, golden rain and Roman candles gushed from the trunk, and, at last, the whole tub blew up with a gorgeous and shattering report. The girls laughed and clapped their hands. Then another tree was lit, and the naive set piece repeated itself.

Such scenes as this belong to the life of a civilization that is rapidly changing. They have an innocent, spontaneous air about them that cannot long survive the train, the motorcar, the radio, and the press. We can therefore congratulate ourselves that we have destroyed them, for our flat, stale, unprofitable civilization has seduced them from the natural springs of their own ways, so that now they even blush at their own customs, so anxious are they to ape ours.

Yet which is more civilized? To use gunpowder for crackers, or for murder? To listen to the radio, or take your pet thrush out under the willows by the water that it may be happy and you may hear it sing? To rush about madly over the face of the earth in car or aeroplane seeing nothing, or to spend hours in the contemplation of a single flower? We should have little difficulty in choosing, I think, if the general fever to "do" something, to "save time," did not possess us. (And what will you do with the time when you have saved it? Ask the Chinese.)

In any event, whether we congratulate ourselves or not, nothing will now stop the Juggernaut. The Foreign Devils have come with their ships, shells, and aeroplanes, sold them to the East, and taught it their use. The thing has caught on like a deadly virus. There is no antitoxin. A general conflagration is at hand, and it will only be poetic justice if we are hoist with our own petard, for we started it and they are far more numerous than we.

But whoever goes under in the all-round cancelling out, I am certain that China will survive. They know about conquest, they have been conquered before. The Tartars conquered them and were absorbed, the Mongols, the Manchus, even the Jews, have all invaded China in various ways; and always, like a buried tortoise, the shell slowly, ponderously, lifts and emerges again. So I believe Japan, the quickest and malevolent copyist in the world today, will find in the immense inertia of China's four hundred millions a sort of python grip that will ultimately swallow her whole. And then when it is all over someone will set out to recover the lost values and set up the forgotten standards. Civilization is an inward, not an outward thing.

Spring came in a sudden riot. One day you were pulling down your ear-flaps and burrowing into your fur coat, and the next the almond tree in the courtyard had tumbled into flower, the willows had let down their hair, the cherry blossom was bubbling and bursting along the twigs. The temperature had risen twenty degrees: it was as if God had suddenly relented of some punishment against the earth and lifted His hand to let the spring gush forth. In a fortnight everything was in full leaf; the vine had been dug out of its winter mound, the peonies thrust forth their bronze shoots, the lilacs were labouring day and night to perfect their heavy trusses—never have I seen such lilac as Peking can show in May.

Our instruction continued steadily, and now much more comfortably. Some of our pupils had gone solo, some showed signs of developing into decent pilots; but generally speaking, they were very slow. I often wonder now how those first batches were selected, whether the best type of man had been found, or whether, since, a class more fitted has come forward. For, as far as we could see at that time, the chances of a competent Chinese Air Force were extremely slender.

My best pupil was Mr Ma. I grew very fond of him, for he was more alive and eager than the rest. He had a fine sensitive face, full of expression, not bland and impassive as many Chinese faces seem to us to be. His broad square brow was surmounted with a close-fitting cap of hair that stood up one end, short and straight, somehow pleasantly pugnacious, his eyes were level and steady, his cheeks a little drawn, nose (for a Chinese) on the long side, and his mouth and chin trim and firm. He had acquired a few words of English; but, though that made it easier for me, he didn't really need them, for he had the right feel, something every instructor instantly recognizes, the natural ability of a born pilot. It was a pleasure to teach him, and I soon got him off solo. By the summer he flew well, and was the first man we trusted with a Vimy alone, and later he accompanied me on my one and only trip to Tsinanfu.

When the summer wars came on—there was some sort of a small war every summer, it seemed a function of the temperature—he was sent up in a Handley Page. The machine was nothing to do with us, so how or why it happened I never knew; but the great lumbering thing caught fire in the air, and little Mr Ma was burned to death.

The evening started badly, I lost my temper. It was the heat, the nervous irritability that an Englishman, bred to frost and fogs, sometimes gives way to when he lives in the atmosphere of a Turkish bath. To be in a state of copious perspiration day after day, night after night, to feel your shirt sticking to your back, your collar to your neck, your hand to the paper on which you write—all this lacerates your mental balance and, quite suddenly, you rave over something perfectly insignificant. So it was in this case.

I was late back from the Club, due to dine out and drove recklessly along the narrow dusty hutungs, pulled up all standing at my front door and ran in for my white evening kit. Jo, my boy had not put it out. I yelled across the courtyard for him to do it now, at once, and why the devil hadn't he done it before? He hurried in and I jumped into a cold tub. By the time I was rubbed down, everything was lying out on the bed. Now, if you will believe me, the boy had been idiot enough to put me out a stiff shirt! A stiff shirt! With the thermometer at 100 in the shade! Anyone with a grain of sense would have known that I wanted a soft shirt. There were no soft shirts. Well, why not? Why hadn't he seen to it that there was a soft shirt when I wanted one? I had not enough soft shirts. Who was he to tell me how many soft shirts I ought to have? His business was to produce a soft shirt when it was wanted ... And more in the same vein.

I arrived late for dinner. The other guests were drinking a second cocktail in the courtyard. We were to dine out of doors. Two lanterns stood like huge golden balls on the paved ground. The grey brickwork, the vermilion shutters, the paper windows were all overlaid with a fine tracery of tree shadows. Through open doors a distant candle lay mirrored in a polished floor like a lily in a pool. The sickly scent of flowering trees intoxicated the air, which hung heavy and languorous below the tilted eaves.

We sat down. Two boys stole silently about the tables. Dishes appeared and disappeared as if by magic. From time to time above a pale sculptured shoulder of the West a yellow impassive face of the East would appear, turning a menial service into a mystical rite. Dinner wore on and I began to feel the house, the courtyard, the guests, the ghostly servitors had all been conjured into life for this one moment only and would presently dissolve. Conversation flagged. The last blue plate vanished into the shadow. Cigarettes began to glow, lighting for a moment some smooth forehead, brooding eyes that saw nothing, so deep was their repose. Silence came down like something palpable, too heavy to be lifted by a word. Upon one lantern a huge moth explored laboriously the curved surface of its golden world, trembling with wonder at the joys within. Somebody sighed. It was so still I heard my own heart beating …

'If only there were music!' said a low voice at my side; and immediately, as if obeying her will, from the big Bluthner within, the first notes of the Liebestod stole out into the night …

The stage, you perceive, was set. On such a night something was bound to happen. Looking back on it now, I cannot always persuade myself of its reality. Perhaps it was no more than a dream within a dream, and the greater dream itself only a fitful waking in some profound unending sleep. I do not know and, anyway, it does not matter. The voice which seemed to have command over the spirit of music was entirely strange to me. I had never heard it before, and I am fated never to see its owner clearly. The shadows and the candlelight confused my sight. I know the head was dark and shapely, the mouth tragic, the hands cool. So much I retain; but no more. The whole thing is elusive. It might never have happened.

The Walls of Peking stand square about the city. Once polished with the tread of many feet, they now lie deep in weeds, and where once the archers, thumb-ringed with jade, stretched their tall bows, there wanders between tall grasses and flowering nettles a little twisting footpath trodden by few but the curious, the idle, and the solitary.

It was here we came walking when midnight had struck. Within the city a few late lights showed the house-roofs, strange twisted shapes, like the backs of a herd of sleeping cattle; without stretched the vast plain on whose horizon the sky cloth rested lightly, pricked with many stars. Framed in the gatehouse pillars, musty, camphor-scented, the round moon fell slowly to the earth.

So the magic of that too short hour eludes my capture. Words did not make it then, and cannot make it now. There was a curious communion, an understanding without speech, uplifting us to certain knowledge. We could do great things; life was a tool, it lay to the hand, obedient as a chisel in the grasp of Michelangelo. A vision of the heights we might attain, a revelation of our purpose and our power, did we not falter, transported us and held us high, secure, complete. We knew.

The moon went down. We left the high places, came into the streets, and in the courtyard of a strange house we parted. A gracious wind cooled the sultry night a little, silvered the poplar leaves and made them whisper. I bent over her hand and kissed it. It lay passive in mine for a moment, then, with an incomparable movement of head and shoulder, she turned and went in.

I drove home in a trance. Life had meaning, order, purpose— and it was good. Ugly things, most of all Death, were blotted out, yet the sombre angel had been close at my elbow all the night.

I knocked, and the coolie opened, letting me through into the courtyard garden. A breath of perfume from a clump of Japanese lilies rose at my feet. The house beyond was dark, and I paused for a moment to look up at the night sky through the close-leaved cherry trees. Then, out of the corner of my eye, I caught sight of something white moving in the shadow of the veranda. I spun round quickly, startled, and called out, 'Who's there?' No answer. I ran up the steps. The white ghost came out of the shadows and seemed to crumple and sink to a heap at my feet. Half a word, half a sigh came from it. It raised two hands and a pale stricken face. It was Jo, my boy. 'Get up! Get up!' I lifted him. He stumbled to his feet, then hid his face.

I took him inside. No need of words now. Least of all now. The white mourning robe and the heavy turban told their story. But still he blundered: 'You know, Master. My father makee die.' He paused, strangely impassive, I did what I could; little enough; gave him money for the funeral (for a man's place in the world is judged by the pomp of his burial), comforted him in some fashion, I hope, and sent him to bed.

The night was far gone and I had lost all hope of sleep. The order in the shape of things had broken. The brief transfiguration of an hour ago was gone. The veils of mystery, bewilderment came down again and I was back on the old path, groping. A thousand times I reproached myself for stupid anger against a man who, even while I was railing at him, must have been struggling in the depths of bereavement and grief. A thousand times I tried to understand why a moment of revelation had been granted to me, who had no crying need of it, while to him such consolation had been denied. If I believed in Divine Justice or Personal Immortality some balance might at last be struck; but I did not believe in either, so I could not find that easy panacea—fobbing it off on God. It was too great and intricate a pattern for my solving. I knew a vivid conscience could be worse hell than any priest or poet could devise. There stood the limit of my understanding.

∿

At last the shutters turned grey. Day was breaking, I heard the gate open, and knew that Jo was starting on his journey to some little group of pine-shadowed tombs, peaceful in the hollow of the hills. I dressed quickly and passed out, following at a distance. Upon the HaTaMen, a spacious avenue that runs north and south the whole span of the city, a little group of men were waiting. They were dressed in dull green coats with queer black hats, a red feather peaked up from the crown. Some carried banners, others gilded horns. They looked pale and tawdry in the early light, a mockery of grief, clowns aping sorrow. There was no great catafalque with its pall of crimson and its hundred men; this simple box of pine went high on the shoulders of twelve coolies, who stepped out firmly, singing as they went. Behind, a white-covered Peking cart, a white mule and, sitting cross-legged on the shafts, the ghost of last night, shading his eyes with one hand, according to the ritual prescribed. I followed them to the gates, now thronged with barrows of fruit and vegetables from the gardens round about. Their wheels rumbled over the paved tunnel beneath the Wall as that pathetic little train moved out, and one priest clad in an orange robe flung discs of paper high in the air—prayers to defend the spirit of the departed from the menace of evil. I stood and watched them go.

So one more traveller passed beyond the protecting shadow of the dim, dawn-lit city, and young day waked smiling in the eyes of happier men. Beyond the limit of that vast crepuscular horizon the light grew, the earth became radiant with a certain promise of beauty and strength. Life went on! Sweet, truant life, who turns to each of us her face and shows us only what we wish to see, but is no less sorrowful because we laugh, nor less happy because we weep, who goes her own triumphant way, withdrawn, impassive and inscrutable at heart, bidding her guests find in her what they can.

A cloud of white pigeons wheeled above the Wall. Upon their backs the reed flutes whistled merrily. Could it be that same Wall where we had wandered with slow thoughtful steps among the weeds? On what white pillow lay that head? So close, so far away, so dear, yet so estranged by one brief step of time.

The great barrow wheels creaked piteously. The straining coolies, naked to the waist, struggled with their heavy burdens, calling to each other in sharp anxious voices. Then a load of egg plants overturned, and between the quarrelling men the rich fruit lay like globes of amethyst, shining in the dust.

Cecil Lewis in the cockpit

*F*ROM THE OUTSET IT HAD BEEN OUR ambition to inaugurate a commercial service, the first in China, between Peking and Shanghai. The distance was about eight hundred miles. We could do it in three or four hops. The one thing lacking was the aerodrome and the ground organisation, and, though the thing was discussed interminably, it never seemed to mature.

I have already referred to the tortuous Chinese psychology, to the corruption of "squeeze" in official circles, and to the extraordinary lack of anything approaching Western executive or administrative ability. It was really impossible to get anything done, and if it was done you might be sure it would be beautifully bungled.

The whole Chinese system of government used to be based on the Confucian philosophy, ancestor worship, reverence for the head of the family, which, politically, established a train of respect or responsibility, according as to whether you looked up or down the scale, from the father of the meanest family to the village headman, from him to the head of the district, and so on, in widening circles, up to the Governors of the Provinces, who were directly responsible to the Emperor himself. The difficulties, owing to the vast size of the country and the teeming population, must have been many; but in the golden days of China's greatness it seems to have worked as well as any other political system, that is to say, adequately, with no more than the usual amount of corruption and abuse.

But with the fall of the monarchy the keystone of this elaborate arch was knocked out. There was no final court of appeal of authority. Each provincial governor became a law unto himself, and these men developed later into the warlords, *tuchuns*, each one maintaining a private army, and each manoeuvring to gain the power (and thus the income) of some form of established government. Hence the continual summer wars. Only someone intimately acquainted with Chinese politics could possibly keep pace with the continual re-shufflings and alliances. The intrigue was complex, continual, subterranean. No wonder an official in power feathered his own nest as quickly as he could. Tomorrow he might be out. We often wondered whether the whole aviation contract was not a manoeuvre for someone to acquire a substantial squeeze, for the obstacles, postponements, and lack of any serious attempt to organize seemed difficult to account for otherwise.

So the spring passed in rumours of the start of the service; but nothing happened. The temperature rose daily, the great heat and the two months' rains were at hand; evidently it would all have to be put off till the autumn.

But not a bit. Some change occurred in the political position, some pressure had been brought to bear, and suddenly the service was to be inaugurated forthwith. Needless to say we were furious, for how could you expect to maintain any regularity through the worst period of the year? And what was the good of starting the service at all if you did not mean to keep it up? The ridiculous lack of common sense revolted our Western habit of planned and progressive action. We pointed out that the rains would be hampering and dangerous, that the aerodromes would be flooded, that they had not completed the ground organisation anyway.

But it was useless. If the other aerodromes were una-vailable, the first one, at Tsinanfu, was ready. If the service could not reach Shanghai, it could at least leave Peking. The great thing was to start it. Whether it ended or not was quite beside the point.

∽∶∾

Now, the weather in north China is so regular, and has been observed and recorded by the Chinese for so many hundreds of years, that it is possible to say within a week when the rainy season will begin. They decided to start the service on the very day the first rains were expected! By this time the thing had to be taken as a joke, at which, owing to the temperature, we laughed somewhat shortly. There were the usual inaugural banquets during the few days previous to the send-off, interminable food, interminable speeches, press reporters, bands, flags all over the aerodrome, crowds of people, and at last Pat climbed on board the Vimy and set off on the first flight. Of course the thing was a farce, for there were no passengers, one small bag of mail, and two of our own mechanics in the cabin, while to give the thing more "face" (prestige), Pat took one of his pupils in the second pilot's seat. (I believe it was stated that this Chinese was really flying the machine, and that the Englishman was taken purely as a formality.) The rains held off. Pat reached Tsinanfu, stayed the night and returned the next day. On the day following that I left with Mr Ma, eight ounces of mail, and two mechanics.

Still the rains held off, and although the afternoon was very hot (about 105 in the shade), it was perfect, and at four thousand feet reasonably cool. It was my first and only cross-country flight in China of any extent, and quite an experience, for the ground was entirely devoid of any of the usual landmarks by which a pilot finds his way. Beyond the railway, the Grand Canal, and the Great Wall, there were, at that time, no outstanding features on the surface of north China. There were the Western Hills, which soon slipped behind, and beyond this nothing but a flat featureless plain dotted with innumerable small villages. No roads, no woods, no rivers, nothing but nets of cart-tracks radiating in every direction from each village and connecting it with those about it. A forced landing in such country would find you fifty miles or more from any modern method of transport or communication. Heaven alone knew how you would get yourself or the machine back to civilization. To dismantle it and return in carts seemed the only solution. So I thought as we sailed south-west on a compass course, but did not have to make the experience, for, after three hours, we sighted Tsinanfu, town, river, and aerodrome, came down, put the machine in its shed, and walked into the town to be received into the hospitality of the British Consulate. It was a perfect evening. Where were the promised rains?

They started that night. A violent thunderstorm and cloud-burst, a gushing rattling deluge that streamed from the roofs and slashed against the panes. This sort of rain has to be seen to be believed. Nothing of the kind ever visits England. It is as if there was water above the heavens, and someone had pulled out a slide, loosening a cataract solid on to the earth. At daybreak they stopped. The sun came out. The Consulate was well drained, so that the amount of water that had come down did not at first appear. I was warned against trying to get to the aerodrome. It was out of the question to fly, the rains would return in the afternoon; but there was the schedule to be maintained, however futile the whole thing might be. If I possibly could, I must get the machine off and return to Peking.

꘎꘎

So we set out. Soon the difficulties began to appear. The tracks were flooded, the fields were lakes; but by making some detours, walking on the mounds by ditches, we progressed slowly for a little until we were brought to a real full stop.

Through a slight dip in the ground ran a raging yellow torrent, about a hundred feet across, rushing past at six miles an hour. We stood there contemplating it, baffled. Evidently we should have to go back. There was no way across this except by swimming.

At that moment on the far side a coolie appeared, gesticulating and shouting something. He waded into the water, pushing a small tub, about the size of an earthenware bread bin, before him. He crossed towards us, the water up to his neck, reached the shallows, and emerged, chattering at Mr Ma.

'He invites you, sir,' said Mr Ma, 'to cross in this small boat.'

The small boat was made of wicker, roughly lacquered with mud, reasonably water-tight; but it was not big enough to float anything larger than a six months' baby. Now I weigh 13 stones and stand 6 feet 4 inches. The "boat" would reach perhaps half-way up to my calves, and my two feet, if curled up, might just find place on the bottom. I thought the thing impossible, and the idea of being tipped out into the swirling yellow water failed, at that moment, to appeal to my sense of humour. I suggested Mr Ma should make the experiment. He entered the tub without hesitation, while the coolie held it steady, and resting his hand on the man's head, was ferried across without incident.

It was my turn next. If you have ever tried to stand upright in a small canoe, you know how it wobbles from side to side. This "small boat" wobbled that way in all directions. I half stood, half crouched, clutching the coolie's pigtail to steady myself, and we launched away. It must, from the way the two mechanics laughed, have been a ridiculous sight. My weight sunk the tub almost to the brim. The coolie, stepping uncertainly on the muddy bottom, slid this way and that, time and time again we were on the point of being overset. But he was a stout fellow that coolie. He pushed, he swore, he laughed, he slithered (and, Lord, how he smelt!); but at last we were safely across, and I stood triumphant on the far bank encouraging the others to follow.

Now the tub had been in none too strong a condition at the outset, and the journeys had weakened it, so that by the time Bill—our best Rolls Royce mechanic—came to cross, last, it was definitely leaky. Half-way across, the bottom fell out. Bill, with a curse, fell through to the mud beneath. The coolie hooted with laughter, but stuck on to Bill, assisting him through the shallows, and he emerged, wearing the tub round his middle, like a serviette ring, and using very colourful language. While he wrung out his ducks we paid off the coolie, to whom the loss of the tub seemed of no importance, and then proceeded. Soon we came to a small lake. 'No more of them bloody tubs for me,' said Bill.

Then, from a house appeared, I have always wondered how, four Chinese ponies, saddled and bridled. Their owner invited us to mount. Now I had been bitten in my childhood by a horse, and therefore agreed with Maurice Beck, who, after twenty years in China, gave his considered opinion on the Mongol pony very succinctly: 'Nasty vicious animals: one end bites the other end kicks.' However, once again there was nothing else for it. We mounted into the hard wooden saddles, stuck our feet in the heavy brass stirrups, and trotted off—I, like the White Knight, on the point of overbalancing at every step. At length we reached the aerodrome. It had taken us two hours to do our twenty-minute walk of yesterday.

Half the aerodrome was a soggy marsh. The machine, in the shed, was pretty well bogged. But there was a strip, higher than the rest, which might, I thought, serve to take off from, if we could get the machine to it. We started the engines up in the shed and managed to taxi out, but at once the wheels sank up to their axles, and full power from both engines (600 b.h.p.) refused to budge it an inch. A gang of coolies appeared—these things always seemed magical—and fifty were placed under the leading spar of each lower wing. They crouched and raised the spar with their shoulders, then, with both engines at full throttle, foot by foot, she moved slowly forward on to the better ground.

I suppose it was foolhardy ever to have made the attempt at all. On the other hand, the rains might last six weeks, and a week in this humidity and temperature would have been enough to turn the machine green with mildew, so leaving the men and Mr Ma to return by train, and taking advantage of every inch of run, I opened up. She crawled along, gradually gathering way, got up to about thirty miles an hour, and then we came to the end of the good ground. I closed the throttles, she sank, stuck, and turned up on her nose. So that was that.

We threw a rope over the tail and pulled it down. Luckily there was little damage, for the nose of the Vimy had a small wheel to protect it against such accidents. Laboriously we hauled the machine back to the start of the run again, and decided to leave it at that for the day. In the interim we got cinders put down, and the strip of ground stamped firm by coolies. But it was two days before the Vimy could be got off and flown back to Peking. And that, for the year 1921, was the end of the Peking–Shanghai Air Service.

The Empress Dowager posed as the Goddess of Mercy.
Yu, Court Photographer, 1912.

*B*EFORE COMING OUT TO China, I had heard vaguely about something called the Boxer Rising, something about ' troubles' in Peking. But what the rising was and what the troubles were, I never dreamed of finding out. The China I dreamed about was far away, mystical, romantic, beautiful. I had just come through the War, remember, and anything ugly, anything about violence or killing was now, thank God, over and done with.

I was going to China to do a job, but that was routine. What I really dreamed of—hardly knowing it—was a sort of hunger for some other way of life which I felt would hold more promise for me than anything I had found here, at home. It was all very adolescent, childish in a way; but I do not now, in old age, at all regret it. It belonged to those years when all life was before me, unknown, exhilarating, exciting and I wanted it to be as I dreamed of it, a sort of saga to be lived. Impossible, of course— yet, in a way that is how it has turned out—in spite of all my failures, mistakes and short-comings, I can sometimes put all the wrongs in brackets, as it were, and only see the exhilarating luck and joy that God has given me.

That was certainly how I felt when, at last I got to Peking and began to get the flavour and atmosphere of that remarkable and unique city. It was full, over-full, of all the excesses and dreams, of all the unexpected, ridiculous and magical hopes I had had of it.

So I cannot pretend, in remembering so much of my days in Peking, that the Boxer Rising had any part in it. It came up in conversation, of course: how this had been burned down, how that had been looted, how something else had been destroyed; but it was all ugly, to be pushed aside, forgotten.

Yet I was certainly talking to some people who had been there, had survived the siege of Peking, had seen the horrors and atrocities committed around them. Their lives or deaths seemed to have rested on a series of lucky breaks, in which bravery, stupidity, determination and ignorance were all mixed up, as I suppose they are in all wars, but it had all 'come out' all right. So the whole thing, now it was twenty years in the past, was best forgotten.

But later, when I began to look back on those days I found I became quickly engrossed and captivated by the sudden unexpected outburst of events which had almost wrecked all foreign interests in China.

In retrospect it was only a hiccup in the ruthless game of greed and grab the West was playing to take over huge slices of the East and grow rich on it. It was wholesale theft, of course, but under the name of religion, education and 'civilization' all the sham and crockery was brushed under the carpet—only to be found out half a century later.

Sometimes in conversation with my friends, my age comes up, and we contrast life today with life in the days of my childhood and youth. How I remember my first ride in a steam driven motorcar, how the train was a national wonder, how the first telephone—to speak to people who weren't there—was magic. Through a wire! How could speaking go through a wire? Impossible.

The West had certainly made 'advances' by the use of techniques which cowed and frightened 'natives' who were slaughtered when they tried to defend themselves and the old ways. But we had not reached the days when one country could threaten to destroy the world. There were situations around the turn of the century when these new techniques could not annihilate time and distance and get you through emergency crises.

Then those who were trapped began to realise, for the first time, what life was like when long distance communication failed, what it meant to be cut off, unable to tell people far away what has happened, how to get help you desperately need when you can't reach the helper, how all the simplest needs are made a thousand times more difficult—and even more frustrating when those who could help don't even know you are in difficulties nor what help you want.

Suddenly you are alone. You have to rely on yourself. You have to take decisions, without advice, without someone to fall back on, when your place in life seems knocked from under you. These are the times when leaders appear, when people in perhaps quite secondary positions turn out to be the only ones who can really see the essentials, what must come first, what must be done and how to do it.

This certainly was the case in Peking at the time of the Boxer uprising when British, German, French, Russian, American, Japanese and Austrian legation staffs, and indeed all western people and Christian converts were trapped, faced with sudden death. With the telephone lines cut, railway lines smashed and nobody in the outside world knowing anything about it, even knowing they were in trouble!

Who were these maniacs, these 'Boxers' who were burning all aliens alive, over a thousand of them, just because they were foreign devils, Christians and enemies of China?

The Boxer Rising first flared up in Shantung, where a group of peasants suddenly attacked and murdered the foreigners and missionaries working among them.

This local outbreak suddenly caught on and flared up in other parts of China where foreigners, for various reasons had been allowed to trade in China and had introduced western inventions which changed the age-old customs and ways in the life of the East and began to infuriate them.

It was the inevitable result of the new intruding on the old. The nineteenth century was a time when the West began to develop the practical inventions of 'science' and bring them into general use. Trains and the telegraph and modern firearms were the start of 'the new civilization'.

The West had brought in these novelties partly to improve the life of the 'natives', but also to conquer them, and rule over huge additions to their 'Empires'. China was the first to see this was an attack on their way of life—and violently rejected it. All modernity was the work of the devil. It was a strong subconscious feeling that if China was to survive she must act now before she was swamped by the evil spirits of the foreign devils.

The foreigners, particularly the British, could not understand this. They viewed colonization as paternal care. They were simply showing backward children, the way to a better life. Their petulant outbursts could not be taken seriously. Very soon they would see it was childish to get angry about the very things that were being introduced to help them. Of course they had to be governed and obey. This was what made it all work. Soon they would reap the advantages of all these novelties and prosper.

Being simple people they believed all this and at first submitted. But they were deeply attached to their old ways of life and when the West rode roughshod over them, they began to rebel. It was some time before the foreigners took this deep growl of rejection seriously. But as the brutal murders of missionaries and their Chinese converts spread and hordes of violent fanatics burned Catholics and their churches, not only around Peking but also down at Tientsin, the port nearest them on the coast, they reluctantly began to see it was time to 'do something' about it.

These outbreaks, of course, affected all foreign nationals in Peking, at least eight nations and, as usual, they could not agree on joint action. A vital period of time was wasted in various attempts to get help to them, but when this failed the Peking Legations began to realize they were completely cut off. It had only taken six months since the first rumour of trouble with the Boxers had been heard from Shantung in January 1900 till the moment on June 20th when the British Legation and the whole Legation Quarter of Peking finally realised it was trapped, surrounded and facing murder and annihilation.

Of all this people back in Europe were quite unaware and the shock of the news when, at last, it reached them was traumatic, made worse by the realisation that they could do nothing about it. No modern inventions could help in this. It would take weeks for any ship to get to Tientsin and months before any relieving force could be organised to raise the siege of the Legations in Peking itself.

The total number of nationals living in the Legation Quarter was about 800, including women and children and a few Chinese gardeners, workmen and servants. The active defending 'manpower' of all legation staffs was put at 400 men: plus about 150 armed volunteers. They had no reserves of ammunition, since each country had different firearms. They had four pieces of light artillery and a small assortment of automatic weapons. Their only assets were five good wells, a sufficient supply of food and animals—and plenty of courage.

The 'enemy' consisted of endless hordes of angry violent peasants, convinced they were immune to firearms, fearless, lightly armed, almost totally unorganised, undisciplined, but madly determined to murder or burn every foreign devil in China.

The government of China had collapsed under the ineptitude and ignorance of decadent Emperors. All requests by the besieged foreign Ministers asking for government assistance in restoring order remained unanswered. The self-appointed Dowager Empress who ruled by decree, dexterity and determination had no intention of helping the foreign devils.

There was evidently disorder among the Chinese. Even after the first week of furious attacks on all the Legations, suddenly about four o'clock one afternoon, a horn sounded and all firing stopped! When this astonishing silence continued till evening, one of the defenders in the British Legation decided to make a careful recce of the enemy lines. From a point of vantage over the walls of a burnt-out house, he described an extraordinary scene:

> The sun's slanting rays now struck the Imperial City. Just outside the Palace gates were crowds of Manchu and Chinese soldiery, infantry, cavalry and gunners grouped together in one vast mass of colour. Never in my life have I seen such a wonderful panorama—such a brilliant blaze in such rude and barbaric surroundings. There were jackets and tunics of every colour; trousers of blood-red embroidered with black dragons: great two-handed swords in some hands; men armed with bows and arrows mixing with Tung Fu-hsiang's Hansu horsemen, who had the most modern carbines slung across their backs. There were blue banners, yellow banners embroidered with black, white and red flags, both triangular and square, all presented in a jumble to our wondering eyes. The Kansu soldiery of Tung Fu-hsiang's command were easy to pick out from amongst the milder-looking Peking Banner troops. Tanned almost to the colour of chocolate by years of campaigning in the sun, of sturdy and muscular physique these men who desired to be our butchers showed by their aspect what little pity we should meet if they were allowed to break in on us. Men from all the Peking Banners seemed to be there with their plain bordered jackets showing their divisions but of Boxers there was not a sign.

The truce lasted all evening and the besieged hoped it might mean some change of plan. But we heard later that the Empress, if she had changed her plans, changed them again. Furious with her generals for stopping the attack, she raved that she was going to 'eat the flesh and sleep on the skins of the foreigners.' A heavy attack on the Legations was resumed at midnight.

The Dowager Empress was a headstrong absolute ruler, but she had no idea about military matters. If she ordered people to be destroyed, they would be destroyed. Her people would see to it. She was perhaps the last patriot of old-time China, power-less, but cunning, a double-faced mistress of dissembly and delay. At first she ignored the Boxers, but later, seeing they might be of help to China, she began to help them by giving them the support of the army, unofficially. Publicly, during all this time, she remained neutral, pretending to be free of all involvement, knowing this would help in making terms with the detested foreigners later, when all this was over.

Admiral Sir Edward Seymour was the leader of the expedition which set out to relieve the Embassies in Peking. News that his train, in five sections, with two thousand men, had left Tientsin was one of the last messages received in the Legation before all communications were cut. As it was only a five hour journey relief was expected soon and this did a lot to relieve anxiety in the Legations during the first days of the siege.

But in fact the Boxers had severely damaged the railway. Rails and sleepers had been lifted and burned and it took the convoy two days to cover half the distance and reach a village called Lofa. Here the train, with a force of about 2,000 allied troops, was fiercely attacked by the Boxers on the third day and this was followed by further attacks. All these attacks were beaten off, but at considerable cost.

Now Seymour, only 30 miles from Peking, was forced to see that advance along the railway was impossible and he must fall back on an alternative plan of proceeding up the river Pei Ho. But when another section of the train was heavily attacked by a force of 4,000 Chinese regular troops, Seymour realised he had to deal with more than the Boxers. His forces were outnumbered, strung out and he had lost touch with his base, the allies' naval forces off the coast. The whole of north China had become a trap.

Then, luckily, in a brilliant action, the allied navies attacked and overpowered the Chinese coastal forts. The river approaches to Tientsin were opened. Troops and supplies could be landed, foreign forces strengthened. The whole situation seemed reversed.

All this was, of course, quite unknown to the besieged in Peking. Their conditions deteriorated rapidly. It was the summer period of intense heat, but Legation staff felt it their duty to sally out and bring in as many Christians from the city as they could. They might be massacred at any moment. In this they were more lucky and successful than they had dared to hope, but these refugees put a big strain on the Legation. How were they to find living space to feed and care for several thousand frightened people utterly disorientated and terrified at the imminent prospect of death?

But, in fact, these refugees proved an enormous asset. They helped to put the Legation on a siege basis. They fetched and carried, cooked, washed and cleared up. The women sewed hundreds of sandbags made from every sort of material, sheets, curtains, dresses, anything to strengthen the defences. Altogether they took a huge load off the fighting men who had to man the frail perimeter day and night.

The greatest danger was the Tartar Wall, the south wall of the city, which overlooked the German, American and Dutch Legations. If the Boxers got control of the wall, all these legations would be at the mercy of the attackers above them and would certainly be wiped out.

But a small force of Germans and Americans made a dashing sortie along the wall top and drove back the attackers as far as the Ch'ien Men, the central South Gate. A gang of Christian converts came up behind and built rough but solid barricades, enough to enable the wall to be held. The greatest danger was averted, but the cost was heavy, filling the two rooms, called the hospital, almost without medicines, anaesthetics and bandages, with over sixty casualties.

Another sortie was made by the British on the labyrinth of burning houses which overlooked the legation defences and the Japanese also cleared another dangerous area. The defenders had now done all they could to secure their position. All they hoped was to hold on till they were relieved.

As in all such high risk conditions, the days were full of incident, rumour, danger, terror and boredom. On the whole the morale seems to have been wonderfully steady. But the constant threat remained. The city wall was the most vital and difficult to hold. It was lost and regained again and again, but somehow it was held.

Every day had its surprises. Non-existent searchlights were seen. Remarkable, improbable contacts with the outside world kept their spirits up. The entire garrison lived on a stream of rumours of almost immediate relief, all of which proved quite false. There were mines, explosions. There was a madman who got out and when he was caught by the Boxers gave them masses of misinformation. There was the splendid building of Betsey, the weirdest home-made field gun any company of army engineers ever put together. There was the tragic burning down of the Hanlin library of antique Chinese books said to be the finest in the world just beyond the north wall of the British Legation. There was ... the list of incidents is endless. The whole place lived on hope. And the days dragged on and on ...

The siege of the Peking Legations lasted 55 days. The reason no help could quickly be brought to Peking was the way the Boxer menace had flared up over the whole of North China. Tientsin town itself had become a fortified walled city which had to be overpowered before any question of a move north-ward could even be thought of.

This in itself proved a difficult and costly business and Tientsin did not surrender until July the 15th. By then Peking had been under siege for more than a month and no attempt at relief had even been thought of.

Volunteers carrying messages giving details of the state of the siege had been sent out from Peking. None had returned, but, at last, a boy of fifteen, who had slipped out with a begging bowl, got back on July 28th with a message sewn into the collar of his coat. It read:

> A mixed division of 2,400 Japanese, 4,000 Russians, 1,200 British, 1,500 Americans, 1,500 French and 300 Germans leave Tientsin on or about July 20 for the relief of Peking.

Naturally this news was received with great joy by the besieged. The prospect of early relief from their ordeal was wonderful. But there was still a long wait to come.

The business of organising an international relief force was, as we know all too well today, a long and complex business. Besides the atmosphere had changed. The allies' urgent need to raise the siege had lost its first big hearted drive. The Chinese also were having second thoughts. The value of a murdering horde of wild unorganised peasants, now it had achieved no real success, began to be a doubtful asset to the Dowager Empress.

Meanwhile the crisis in Peking still held the headlines of the British press and filled the Monarchies of Europe with hysterical concern. The papers headlined with wild, unconfirmed horror stories of murder and sudden death. The climax of these came from a Daily Mail correspondent who, when he finally reached Shanghai, filed a lurid story headed 'The Peking Massacre'—the entire British Legation staff had been wiped out. This dreadful news prompted a memorial service in St Paul's—

quickly cancelled when other less overwritten dispatches reached the capital. Nevertheless the situation in Peking was now really desperate. The relieving forces were still delayed. The Peking defenders were almost without ammunition, worn out by heavy losses and fatigue.

But, unknown to them, there were other 'behind the scenes' forces at work. Chinese Princes and other official advisers realised this freak unorganised uprising could do no good to China. Semi-official messages hinting at a truce reached the defenders. Gradually the cross firing became less fierce and grew intermittent. On July 15th it just petered out.

This truce was a curious untidy pause in hostilities. The allied relieving forces were still fighting their way up to Peking, arguing about status and priorities. Within the city, while some Boxers were fraternising with the defenders, sudden violent attacks followed and this semi-peaceful hiatus was not finally ended till the 'allied' troops, in a childish show of jealousy, had a race to see who could actually get to the Legations first! By using a sewer as a subterfuge, the British managed to win.

So the siege of the Peking Legations finally came to an end on August 20th. After the highly emotional scenes of relief and joy died down, the first thing to follow was a wild outburst of looting and rioting as the foreign troops went on the loose. The Chinese fled before these conquering heroes, looting themselves. Irreplaceable treasures were smashed or burned. What was left was stolen. It took months for anything resembling normal peaceful daily life to come back.

؈

Although, at the time of the siege of the Legations there was a wretched, beaten-down legal Emperor of China, the old Dowager Empress, his aunt, still remained the actual ruler. Feared by all, she had absolute power. Her word was law.

When the Boxer Rising broke out she did nothing to help the foreigners. She seemed to feel herself above all these intruders. She believed that China ruled the world and she ruled China. Everything she thought and did was right and could not be questioned. This absolute, single-minded patriotism led her to hate and wish to destroy all foreigners as the enemies of China. At the same time to come down to their level and fight them would be beneath her.

Although China had already been defeated in clashes with Japan and France, she had taken no steps whatever to build an armoury or guard her frontiers. She simply did not understand the powers in the outside world or know how to meet them.

But perhaps, she may have thought, these Boxers who had the same patriotic ideals as she had, perhaps they could do for the country what she could not do? It was worth a try. So, pretending to stand above it all, she privately supported the Boxers with her army. But when she saw the whole of that shameful and horrible murder of thousands of innocent men and women come to nothing and China was beaten again, she did what she had done before—ran away.

That she might have to run was a possibility, one would have thought, to be considered during the long weeks of the siege. But nobody in the Chinese Court had given it any thought whatever. No preparations had been made. The whole escape was a sudden lunatic scramble, a frantic terrified panic, improvised on the spur of the moment.

The Empress shouted for peasant clothes, cut her nails, plastered down her hair, hid her jewels, called for her frightened Counsellors and poor imprisoned puppet Emperor, Kwang Tsu, stripped him of his pearl-studded coat, told eunuchs to get coolie clothes for him, and for all of them, directed others to collect carts, ponies, drivers, coolies, at the West Gate.

When the Imperial Concubines appeared to pay their respects, they were told they would not be going, and when the

Pearl Concubine dared to suggest that she and the Emperor, whom she loved, should stay in the City, the Empress, despite the frantic entreaties of the half-mad Emperor, shouted: 'Throw this wretched minion down the well'. When this final horrible murder had been committed, leaving her own private quarters, and indeed the whole Forbidden City wide open to looters, the Imperial rabble escaped from Peking in the direction of Sian.

A few days later, a British diplomat's wife went to see the famous sumptuous imperial quarters of the Empress and wrote:

> Her room was just as she had left it. Over the coverlet of the bed lay an embroidered coat of black satin, beneath a pair of Manchu shoes. Nearby were two large boxes of silk handkerchiefs, one pale yellow the other pale blue. In the adjoining room were huge camphor wood boxes, filled with top coats and trousers of every colour, embroidered with gold and pearls. In other boxes were rich sable coats lined with white fox fur ... On a long table were dozens of foreign clocks, some handsome, others hideous, all ticking cheerfully, regardless of the ominous silence all around.

Two days later on a road to the north a Magistrate of a small town met the Imperial fugitives. It was raining. They were sitting by the roadside, wet and cold 'like dejected jackals', parched with thirst and hunger. The wells were full of decapitated heads and the Boxers had stripped the crops from the whole countryside. There was nothing to eat or drink.

The Magistrate managed to procure a bowl of coarse porridge and one pair of chopsticks.

'Who could ever have believed', said the murderous old Empress, 'that it would come to this.'

⌒∴∾

It was in the early days in the attacks on the Legations that the Boxers set fire to any churches, buildings or shops in the city that were in the hands of foreigners or their religious converts. In this vandalism the richest part of the city, the pearl and jewel shops, the silk, fur, satin and embroidery stores, the great curio shops nearly all that was of the highest value in the city was destroyed.

The fire spread to the Ch'ien Men, the huge central South Gate, the 'front door' of the city, crowned by a hundred-foot-high tower which was opened only to permit the solemn passage of the Emperor on his visits to the Temples of Heaven or Agriculture. This landmark in the history of China had been destroyed by the Boxers in a few hours in a dreadful roar of flame and smoke.

When the 'troubles' were over, rebuilding the great tower was at once begun. The good luck of the city depended on it. As the whole structure was made of wood, the roof alone was an enormous undertaking. Those who saw it say it was a sort of magic the way an immense apparently flimsy bamboo scaffolding was lashed together round the gutted tower on top of the forty foot wall, without a nail being used. Behind it all the rebuilding was carried out. When it was completed the bamboo was just pulled down and burned.

This tower surmounting the South Gate was, in fact, not a tower at all. It was similar to other structures crowning all the nine gates of the city. All of them were just long plain four storey 'houses', built as quarters for the soldiers, the guards who had originally manned the walls. It was their magnificent curling roofs, that made these 'towers' superb.

It is said to come from the memory of the earliest days when people lived in tents, but the idea grew into something far more subtle and has been added to in various ways. The silhouette of these gatetowers was greatly enhanced by adding below the huge main roof two lower roofs, of which only the outer edges were seen. They were like frills or veranda roofs that jutted out of the walls under the main roof. It was as if each had been started when the walls were lower and abandoned when it was decided to build the gates higher. The effect was to give an absolutely distinctive character and majesty to their character and beauty.

Though in the days I saw them, they were just splendid ornaments, empty, unused, a sort of crown above the gates, they had become an accent on the noble proportions of the Peking walls themselves, which are, or were, one of the splendours of the ancient world.

At the time I furnished my house, I went 'Ch'ien Men Wai'— outside the gate—almost daily. It was the busy entrance to the wonderland of the Chinese city and all my warmest memories live around it. In those days I didn't look at maps, I just took the Gate for granted, as a sort of entrance to Aladdin's Cave, and it is only now, in this late hour, that I have examined the details of the gates, their inner and outer parts, the pausing place between the two and the part the Gates have played in the long history of the city.

It was more than a year before the Dowager Empress was to return through this gate in a triumphant procession; a year filled with the usual interminable bickering and argument between the 'great' powers on how to share the spoils. China's total liability was assessed at the sum of £675,000,000, payable over 39 years. But who was to pay it? Who represented China? The Emperor was a puppet. The Empress had no legal rights. Her Ministers were elusive, unreliable and evidently anxious to keep out of any official financial responsibility. Eventually China found eleven Ministers and presented their credentials to the allied representatives and asked for theirs in return. None had any credentials to show! Deadlock.

The allies then asked for certain ringleaders to be handed over for trial and punishment. But this was not China's way of doing things. Two Princes were exiled, two were ordered to commit suicide and two were beheaded. Altogether over a hundred minor officials were sentenced, mostly to death. It seems they assumed the Court would be forced to sacrifice them and all showed a strong sense of loyalty to the Throne. All could easily have escaped. None did.

Eventually, by September a Peace Treaty was signed, over a year after the siege of the Legations had been relieved. But, in spite of the 'victory', at the end of it all, none of the allies gained much benefit from it. In a strange way China emerged without any of the annexations of territory which victorious powers usually exerted on those countries which had been forced 'in their own interests' to accept.

Meanwhile the Imperial Chinese Cortege when it realised it was not being followed and would not be attacked, began to regain its royal demeanour and prestige. The Empress, it seemed, was not to be personally punished or humiliated. No Chinese territory was to be annexed. The indemnity was heavy but it could be met over the years. The Empress could grow her nails, resume her dictatorial ways and the curve of royal life began to move upward.

During her flight she had spent some time tidying up the credentials of the Dynasty. She rehabilitated the memories of five Ministers who had been decapitated, she said the Pearl Concubine had virtuously committed suicide 'unable to catch up with the Court when it had left Peking on its tour of inspection'. She disinherited the Heir Apparent and, by implication reinstalled herself in supreme control. It was a long list of lies which nobody believed and everybody accepted.

By June 1901 it was clear a Peace Treaty would be signed and Her Majesty agreed to return to Peking in the autumn to sign it. The announcement was welcomed throughout China.

The gigantic caravan set out from Sian in October, 1901, in 'entire silence and perfect order', a procession of 2,000 carts and ten thousand flags, an extravagant, barbaric and splendid sight. The long files of animals and men, the caparisoned vehicles, the screech of axles, the blare of trumpets along the bright sunlit roads between the mountains. It seemed that everybody enjoyed the 700 mile journey as if it had been a hunting trip. 'Men looked like ants walking up the hills. A wooden bridge was built over the river. There were no waves, the sky was like a mirror. The houses on the hillsides looked like stars.'

A splendid Dragon Barge was built to cross the Yellow River. The Empress showed much affability to the missionaries who had come to watch her pass. The public would not be forbidden to watch her progress as in the past. Now they were invited—an unprecedented condescension of royal generosity and goodwill.

The last part of the journey was made by train. The Belgians had built the line. This sumptuous 'firecart' was something most of the travellers had never seen before. Bursting with Princes, Grand Councillors, eunuchs, concubines, mules and cooks, upholstered with yellow silk, two thrones, several opium pipes and decorated with valuable curios, the train rattled its way towards Peking.

The Dowager Empress had been in hilarious spirits throughout the trip. Now she became worried about getting to the Ch'ien Men at the hour prescribed by the astrologers. But all went well. The splendid procession proceeded up the way to the famous Ch'ien Men Gate, stopping to perform the usual ceremonies on entering the city.

On a sort of balcony over the half re-built tower over the gate, a crowd of foreigners watched the scene.

> All Peking had collected on top of the Wall. We could not have chosen a better place. First to arrive were the Manchu banner men on their fiery little horses, then came a group of Chinese officials and finally the Imperial Palanquins. These advanced at incredible speed between two ranks of kneeling soldiers. The higher the rank of the person carried, the faster he should go. The Court chairs went as fast as the Tartar cavalry.

In the half-moon courtyard between the outer and inner gates stood the two bronze lions who had been blindfolded so that they should not be disturbed when being moved to this new site. Here also was a tiny temple built up against the wall to burn incense and recite prayers prescribed in the Book of Rites for homecoming.

As she got out of her chair, The Empress Dowager looked up at the smoke blackened walls and saw the rows of foreigners watching her arrival from behind the ramparts above. The eunuchs tried to get her to move on. It was not seemly she should stand in full view of everybody. But she was not to be hurried and continued to stand between her two ladies who held her up under her arms on either side, not because she needed help but because such is the custom in China.

At last she condescended to move, but before entering the temple, she stopped once more and, looking up at us, lifted her closed hands under her chin and made a series of little bows. The effect of this gesture was astonishing. We had all gone up on the wall in the hopes of catching a glance of this terrible Empress, whom the West considered almost as an enemy of the human race. But we had been impressed by the magnificence of the swiftly moving pageant and by the beauty of the picturesque group, by the palanquins of yellow satin flashing with gold. Something told us that the return of the court to Peking was a turning point in history and in our breathless interest we forgot our resentment against the woman responsible for so much evil.

That little bow and the graceful gesture of the closed hands took us by surprise. From all along the wall came, in answer, a spontaneous burst of applause. The Empress Dowager appeared pleased. She remained there a few moments longer, looking up and smiling.

She stood below like a great actress taking her curtain call with all the hazards of an awkward first night behind her, bowing to everyone and to no-one, smiling a secret smile, masking her pride behind a show of humility, savouring the moment.

General Dimitri Leonidovich Horvath

*I*T MUST HAVE BEEN ONE EVENING at the Club. Occasionally I dropped in for a drink coming back from the aerodrome. Unexpectedly one of the Secretaries from the British legation came over and introduced the man who was with him:

'Prince Koudasheff, the Russian Ambassador.'

I was astonished. I even thought it was a joke. But the Prince smiled and extended his hand which I took not knowing quite what to say. I'd never met any Russians at the Club. I didn't even know they belonged. They usually kept to themselves, especially now, since the Revolution. But before I could say anything, the Prince surprised me again:

'Mr Lewis, I believe you are a singer?'

This really shook me. How the hell did he know I was a singer? Must be the K.G.B.

'I'm not. I'm—er—just an amateur. I had Russian friends back in England and one of them tried to teach me to sing a bit.'

But the Prince was smiling broadly:

'Typical English modesty! Well'—his English was perfect— 'I just wondered if you would care to meet some other Russian singers who have just arrived here.'

And before I had time to say 'I'd be delighted', he had turned and was talking to the Secretary:

'I don't know if you'd heard; the Chinese Eastern Railway Secretariat in Harbin has appointed General Dimitri Leonidovich Horvath as their representative here in Peking. The General is an old friend of mine. We were students - together. He is also, I suppose, the most respected Russian in the Eastern area of China. He has been Director of the Chinese Eastern Railway since 1903. Now he's here, with all his family, and his personal staff. They're in the Austrian Legation and, young man'—and he'd turned back to me with a smile—'the General has three very pretty daughters who have beautiful voices and it occurred to me you might like to sing with them…'

All this was a bit out of my depth, but I managed to mutter my thanks and say that, of course, I'd be delighted before he cut in, always very much to the point I must say.

'Good. Then, could you come to the Austrian Legation, say, around six tomorrow evening? I shall be there with the General, I'll introduce you to his family.'

He held out his hand again, always with the same warm smile. But I couldn't help feeling it was more an order than a social invitation. 'So, six o'clock tomorrow?' And he smiled again, turned back to the Secretary, took his arm and walked off with him.

I stood looking after him. I wasn't exactly pleased. I didn't like being ordered about. Who were these Russians, anyway?

Of course we'd heard about Communism. But nobody in Peking ever bothered about the Russians or what they were up to. We knew there had been a revolution, a tremendous social upheaval. But it was vague, far off, didn't affect us. Locally, all foreigners in Peking came from the 'West'. There was a Russian Legation, of course, but nobody knew anybody there. In those days with no radio, no newspapers, news about Russia were rare. Lenin was of no interest to anybody.

But, before leaving England I'd actually met quite a number of Russians, mostly musicians, doctors, singers, writers. I had, by chance, started to learn singing from a Russian, Vladimir Rosing, a tenor who had created quite a stir in London at that time. His little coterie of admirers, who met in that tatty little flat in Baker St., was made up entirely of escapees, or just Russians who had happened to be in the UK at that time or who had

escaped from Russia when the sudden communist take-over
blew up. None of them believed it would happen. All of them
were violently against it. Now they were suddenly lost, helpless,
powerless.

I had quickly made friends with these people. Partly because
of the Russian music which I had never heard before and which
I found romantic, exciting and moving in an absolutely new
way. Partly because of my admiration for Val, the tenor, with a
voice so full of fire and love and tenderness, it gave me an idea of
what singing was and could be and also partly for the free
happy-go-lucky atmosphere of the place. With the world falling
to pieces about their ears, that little group of people seemed
quite free of it all, living in the moment, so dreadfully cut off
from their roots, their families, their dear ones—and most of
them absolutely penniless.

But here, in Peking, at the other side of the world, with all the
inconstancy of youth, I had left all that behind, lost touch with
it, almost forgotten it. Communism had quickly become the
'enemy', an absolutely closed shop—and everything I had heard
about it was terrible, terrifying.

But now here was a whole Russian family, in Peking, sound-
ing rather posh, but evidently in new surroundings and a bit
lost—and with three girls, after all—my heart immediately went
back to those old London friends with enormous sentimentality.
All Russians were my friends. I must go and meet this family, at
once.

So, next day, I found my way to the Austrian Legation, a
huge empty, abandoned looking house in a big walled garden. I
saw a bell in the stone pillar that supported a pair of gates. I
pushed the bell then the gates and walked up towards the door.
Before I got there, it opened and a lovely young girl stood there,
smiling. She was tall and slim in her summer dress and had
masses of hair that hung down to her waist. It wasn't a bit what
I'd expected.

Something happened to me. There was a thump in my chest. If it happened to me today I should have said it was the sign of the start of a heart attack. I suppose it was really.

'Good morning' I managed.

'*Bonjour.*' The eyes were downcast. The voice was clear, but somehow tentative. French. It evidently wasn't her mother tongue. Nor was it mine.

'Prince Koubasheff…' I began to explain.

'*Voulez vous voir mon père?*' It was evidently an effort for her to get it out.

'*Oui.*' My French was rudimentary too. Odd words picked up during the war.

Another pause. But I had to carry it off.

'My French is awful!' I laughed.

She didn't understand English I saw that. She was clearly terribly, terribly shy.

'*Suivez moi.*' She turned and led the way in.

The Prince was there and immediately presented me to the General, Dimitri Leonidovich Horvath, and his wife, Camille.

'This is the young Englishman I've found for you girls!' he laughed over to the girls—who all blushed. So did I. They didn't seem like other girls. They were distant, restrained, like Princesses…

I don't really remember how I met the whole household, nor the names, nor the introductions. I lost count. Endless bowing and shaking hands. There must have been twenty people in the room, crowded round a huge dining table. And in the middle of it stood, like an altar, that symbol of Russian family life—the samovar!

They seemed to accept me as a stranger, without having the least idea who I was. None of them spoke a word of English. It would have to be French. It didn't seem to matter.

'*Moi. Anglais.*' I began.

That seemed to go down all right.

'*Beaucoup ami Russe. Angleterre.*' That was obviously a huge success.

'*Moi.* Aeroplane. *Pilote!*' I flapped my hands and arms about. This must be a joke. It started them all laughing. Evidently I came from outer space. From that moment, as I remember it, we became friends.

Then Mama became hostess again: '*Voici mes filles, Mimi, Doushka* (the one who had led me in) *et Ninka. Je suis Camille, leur mère…*'

'And your name? ' the shy one ventured.

'Cecil'

It was new to them. They repeated it, getting the sound of it. Sezle, Se-zeelle. Soon we were all laughing. Such a ridiculous name! They were happy as children.

Mama made a sign and the girls took me off into another room. There was nothing in it but a big grand piano—and music. Sheet music on top of it, on the floor, on the chairs, all over the place. Russian music! The girls started playing, singing, I knew some of the songs, joined in. It was just like Baker St.! In a moment it seemed we were old friends. Those tunes drew my heart out. They still do. These girls gave the impression of being quite uninterested in anything outside the family circle—and their music. They seemed absolutely innocent, living in the moment. This gave them an air of purity, of magical enchantment and, as an impressionable young man, I was enchanted.

Then Mama came in and took over. She played beautifully and the girls sang better when she played. She showed them off, one by one. Such songs! Such pure free voices! This was the first day of my new life!

⌣∴⌣

It was, though we didn't realise it at the time, the end of the Horvath family life and the General's great career in the service of Russia.

The grand Harbin estate would be broken up. The children separated from their parents and dispersed to the ends of the earth. All that remains is the ninety-year-old memory of Doushka who recalls, as best she can, some flavour of those pre-revolution days and her beloved father's splendid work in the building of Russia.

It was evident, even in boyhood that Dimitri Leonidovich was going to be somebody special. He was full of energy and high spirits, intelligent, interested in everything and took an active part in the family farm and the work of the peasants who looked after it. He loved to work with them and got to know them, understand their difficulties and hardships and through-out his life never forgot what he owed to them.

Before he was really grown up he had joined the army in its fight over the treatment of slaves ruled by the Turks, but when that was over immediately turned to what he saw as the greatest problem of Russia—communication. That meant for him, and many other forward-looking young men, joining the Academy of Engineers.

It was vital for the future of Russia to open up her vast terri-tories. The only way to do that was by railways. Dimitri, from then on, devoted himself to what he saw as his life task.

He gave all his youthful enthusiasm and ability to this, distin-guished himself in his studies and soon became known as a man of particular ability and initiative. He began to master all the techniques of railway building, gradients, embankments, bridges, rolling stock and all the problems that grew from laying down the foundation of a network of railways he dreamed would one day be the bloodstream of Russia! He was chosen to build the Caspian Railway and the success of this led to other pioneer projects. Later he was appointed to build the Turkestan

Railway and became a key figure as one of Russia's true pioneers. This finally led to the Czar appointing him to build and direct the Chinese Eastern Railway.

So, in 1900 the family set up a permanent home in Harbin. The Russians had rented the city from the Chinese—in the same manner as England had rented Hong Kong. Russia had realised her need for an opening to the Pacific and the development of eastern Russia was the key. The need for a man to watch over all these developments must obviously be someone who knew the area well. So General Horvath was appointed as Russia's Plenipotentiary for the Czar over the whole of her far east.

By this time the General had married Camille, of the famous Benois family of artists and she had presented him with six children, three daughters and three sons.

Doushka, the second daughter, often speaks lovingly of her childhood, of their huge family property outside Harbin, with its great house, always under guard, its outbuildings, its laundry, bakery, and cellars. She remembers their farm, with cows, sheep, pigs, and poultry and the stables for the General's horses with its own private racecourse. Finally, for convenience, there was the railway siding built into the estate. Here the General kept his own personal coach and office in which he used to travel over thousands of miles, inspecting the problems and developments of the railways.

The whole family used to take their holidays in this coach, travelling the 15 day journey down to Crimea and the Black Sea where they had six huge properties. Here they used to park the coach near the sea and spend wonderful holidays bathing in 'miles of blue sea and golden sand'.

But by 1917 things were changing. Suddenly Communism had taken hold all over Russia. One morning a Russian soldier asked to see the General. Horvath never refused to see anybody, particularly men belonging to the rank and file. The man had a long talk with the General. Then he produced a gun from his pocket: 'I was sent to shoot you, but'—throwing the pistol on the table—'I can't kill a man like you.'

It was an escape—and a warning. The Russian guard on the house was replaced by Chinese. After further attempts on the General's life, the Chinese authorities realised that the whole family might be assassinated at any moment. So they appointed General Horvath as their Counsellor and Adviser in Peking, putting the ex-Austrian Legation at his disposal.

It was just after their arrival that I met the family.

⌣∴⌣

Harbin had been a life of luxury, grandeur and wealth. But somehow, such is the innocence of youth, the girls grew up taking it all absolutely for granted. They never thought about wealth or position at all. 'We grew up', said Doushka, 'among musicians, singers and painters.' This was all they needed or wanted.

In those days a rich girl's destiny was to find the right man to marry, bear his children, manage her husband's house and entertain his friends. From the husband's point of view, his wife held a quite subsidiary role. A woman needed no training for that. She would do as wives had done for ages and a man did not give it any attention. The girl's mother would have taught her daughter what was necessary. It was largely a matter of managing the servants and having a good cook.

It was almost unheard of for a man to discuss his affairs with his wife. What could she know of business? Knowledge of all the 'important' things of life were beyond her. Even further beyond her were any wider, deeper questions of philosophy, psychology, art or religion.

In 1920 when I was a boy of twenty-two, I had been through four years of war. I had seen 'life', I had been educated at a 'public' school, I was an RAF pilot, an officer and I belonged to a certain class of society. The views I have expressed in the above paragraphs were the 'ordinary' views of the 'class' society in which I had grown up. I had never really thought about them at all.

But walking away from the Horvath family that evening my head was in a whirl. I was suddenly confronted, for the first time in my life, with something quite different—a happy family! It seems simple enough but I had never known anything like it. I was an only child. My father was always immersed in his sermons and at the time when I needed a family, my father and mother were breaking the family up. So this sudden burst of happiness quite swept me off my feet with all sorts of ideas, dreams, imaginations, hopes. This was a new and wonderful way of life for me.

I had taken a few girls to bed in a casual light-hearted way. They had made me a gift and I had enjoyed it very much as one enjoys a good meal or a movie. But I was not involved—but now? This was quite different. I wanted to be involved—but how? I wanted to be with this family, this circle of happiness and, most of all, with Doushka, that strange secret lovely girl—tomorrow—and tomorrow—and all the days ahead. I planned how we would go to the markets, to the Summer Palace, to the hills. My head bubbled with possibilities…. The great mirage had arrived, alas! I was in love.

Aerial picture of the Summer Palace

*I*N THE EARLY SPRING OF 1902 the Empress returned in State to the Forbidden City to receive the representatives of the foreign powers and sign the Peace Treaty. But as soon as spring came, she announced that the City would no longer be her place of residence. She removed her Court and all her personal things to the Summer Palace which had been suitably prepared to receive her.

The Forbidden City had tremendous presence and dignity. To enter it, pass the Spirit Screens, cross the great courtyards, gate beyond gate, to stand on the Dragon Pavement and be received into the Hall of Supreme Harmony was very impressive—but it was also a tedious endless ceremony in hot weather.

To live through one summer in China is quite enough to understand this very well and the Chinese Emperors, from the earliest days, have always built themselves summer retreats outside the city, finding cool places with water to escape the heat. The existence of a spring, called the Jade Fountain, a few miles west of Peking, centuries ago was enough to start the building of a succession of palaces there, often destroyed, enlarged and rebuilt down the centuries. The last one left standing when I was there was, as I remember it, a wonderful restful secret of beauty and peace.

The Summer Palace was only a few miles from Peking on the road towards the Western Hills and as I drove along it, I noticed, just before reaching the entrance to the Palace, a lot of ruins, old buildings that had evidently been discarded or pulled down. It was only when I began to write this book and try to bring back so much in those far off days I had mislaid in my memory that it all came back—those ruins were the remains of the original summer palace that the British had destroyed in 1850.

Nobody remembers when the original Jade Fountain spring was first made into a Royal retreat. It certainly existed before the Emperors Kand Shi and Ch'ien Lung enlarged and beautified it in the early days of the seventeenth century. A visiting priest described his memory of it then:

> In his country house outside the capital the Emperor passes the greater part of the year and he works day and night to further beautify it. To form any idea of it one must recall those enchanted gardens which authors of vivid imagination have described so beautifully. Canals winding between artificial mountains form a network through the grounds. In some places passing over rocks, then expanding into lovely lakes bordered by marble terraces. Devious paths lead to enchanting dwelling pavilions and spacious halls of audience, some on the water's edge, others in the slopes of hills or in pleasant valleys fragrant with flowering trees. Within the house may be found all that is curious and rare—a great and rich collection of furniture, ornaments, pictures, precious woods, porcelains, silks and gold and silver stuffs. Nothing can compare with these gardens which are indeed an earthly paradise.

Now, where is this earthly paradise—the Palace of Contentment, the Palace of Floating Clouds, the Pavilion of Favourites—that once ravished the eye? Nothing left but a ruin of rage and destruction. The Great Powers have arrived on the scene.

In 1837 British traders drew up a document to conclude their differences in the export of opium. They failed to agree and this squabble started what was called The First Opium War. But the Manchu government never got around to signing this. So in

1856, together with France, the British declared a Second Opium War on China. An Anglo-French Expedition invaded North China, occupied Tientsin and advanced to within 10 miles of Peking.

Negotiations were begun, but differences again arose. The Chinese considered the allied 'foreign devils' intransigent. They grew more and more irritated and finally the Emperor issued this edict against all foreigners:

> Hereby we make the following rewards: For the head of a black barbarian (Indian Trooper) 50 taels, for the head of white barbarian 100 taels, for the capture of a barbarian leader, alive or dead, 500 taels, for the seizure or destruction of a barbarian vessel, 5,000 taels… We now command that all treaty ports be closed and all trade with France and England stopped. Subjects of other submissive states are not to be molested. When French or English repent of their evil ways and return to their allegiances, we shall be pleased to permit them to trade again as of old so that our Clemency may be made manifest…

As an opening move on these Franco-British 'negotiators' the Chinese arrested 39 members of the allied party. In retaliation, on October the 6th, the allied forces attacked the Summer Palace and pillaged its treasures. The Chinese then agreed to open the gates of Peking and to return their prisoners. It was then found that twenty had been murdered or died from the ghastly prison conditions.

Infuriated, Lord Elgin ordered the burning of the Summer Palace. Maddened by the murder and torture of their own people, the soldiers' onslaught was sudden and thorough. On October 19th, 1860, the Summer Palace was totally destroyed and in wholesale looting of irreplaceable treasures the royal collections disappeared for ever.

The Emperor Hsien Feng, who had issued the edict against foreigners, and his child wife, only just escaped from the

Summer Palace at the last moment—an experience which the child, who grew to be the Dowager Empress, was to repeat when she fled the Forbidden City at the end of the Boxer Rising, fifty years later.

When I first visited the Summer Palace in 1921, I remember the long walkway under a beautiful roof into the first courtyard. It was guarded by a splendid bronze dragon and led to a group of pavilions and courtyards built alongside an artificial lake, which had been enlarged comparatively recently in an unexpected way.

The Western powers, to smooth things over with the difficult Chinese, after the Boxer Rising, offered to present China with a battleship, a start to her proposed new fleet. The Empress Dowager, hating all the 'foreign devils' who had invaded her country, told them that China was perfectly capable of building its own battleship, but would consider accepting a contribution towards it. So the patient and generous West put a sum of several hundred thousand pounds at China's disposal for her to do this.

Once in possession of the money, the Empress scoffed at the very idea of wasting it on building a battleship. Who wanted battleships? China was a peaceful country. Franco-British troops had looted and destroyed the Summer Palace in 1860. Here was an opportunity for a well deserved revenge. She appropriated the whole sum to rebuild and beautify the Summer Palace!

For posterity and its tourists, it was an inspired decision. The pool before the old Palace was enlarged into a fine lake. Courtyards and covered walkways were added to open up more spacious pavilions, to say nothing of a *marble boat* moored to the lakeside—so much more pleasant for taking tea than making war. So the old termagant preserved her dignity, her disposition and the honour of her country until her death.

In her last years she created an entirely new Summer Palace, incorporating the remnants of what had been built by Ch'ien Lung 250 years before. Sumptuous personal quarters, an Audience Chamber, a Reception Hall, a theatre and beautiful gardens, all this was a feat of planning, conceived and carried out by the Empress alone in a space of ten years! The unique traumatic result is perhaps the only noble memory the old devil left to posterity.

Vivid memories are recorded of the great preparations made for the gala days at the yearly reception when ladies, representatives of Foreign Legations, after bitter heartburns and wild scrambles, were finally selected to be received into the Presence of the Empress.

At the Summer Palace silk awnings shaded the verandas and the marble steps were covered with red carpet. When the guests arrived they were led to a pavilion adjacent to the Audience Hall where they arranged themselves in the order in which they were to be presented. Then a double line of Princesses led by the Princess Imperial met them on the marble platform and turned to precede them into the Audience Hall. Here they separated and stood in a picturesque group on either side of the Throne.

The Empress, with the Emperor (her cousin) on her left, were seated on a dais on which was a table, covered with imperial yellow silk flowing to the ground. On it stood exquisite porcelain vases of fruit and flowers.

The foreign ladies made three reverences on entering. After formal presentations had been made, the Empress Dowager descended from the Throne. A cushioned chair covered in yellow satin was brought and, supported by her ladies, she seated herself on one side of the Audience Hall. The ladies were then collectively presented to her. Tea was ordered and the Empress (through an interpreter) said a few words to each.

The ladies were then conducted by eunuchs and the Princesses across the court of the Old Buddha to the pavilion where luncheon was served. A row on the lake in one of the state barges or a performance in the three-storied theatre filled the afternoon. Then the ladies took leave of Her Majesty and were conducted to their chairs or carriages to leave for Peking.

❦

When I had the great good fortune to wander about in all the creations of this wonderful past and the monuments that China has left as records of her civilization, there was one thing I could never understand or believe—the attitude of the common people of China towards their rulers. For centuries they looked upon their Emperors as divine and offered them homage and obedience to a degree quite impossible for us westerners to understand. Even when I was there, China was only just emerging from the Middle Ages.

Such an account as this, for instance, seems absolutely incredible:

> Before he left his Palace the first Drum had sounded and flags were put up along his route, reserving it for the coming of the Majesty. Another Drum and people were directed to go inside, close their doors and windows. Silk curtains were hung to shut off cross roads, while Princes and Officials supervised the laying of golden sand spread on the road before the coming of the Son of Heaven. Another Drum and the Knights in their robes knelt by the roadside to greet their passing Lord.
>
> When at last his Sacred Majesty reached the appointed place of audience he was given an extraordinary reception. Before him silken banners were lifted to the sun, patterned embroideries of many colours, the glory of the Emperor and his ancestors; banners round and square, banners blue and crimson, white cylindrical banners whose story never ends, borne by slant-eyed men in silken coats aflare like rainbows.

Here are those bringing gifts. In the hand of one is a bowl glazed with the blue of forgotten seas; another holds high a long-necked silver swan, tall in its pride. In the carved box carried by a third is rolled a landscape painted in powder of malachite and lapis lazuli, another brings a vase pictured with ladies of an ancient reign—court ladies in trellised gardens, with kingfisher-feather ornaments in their hair and rich robes entwining their slow little feet. Others bear precious charms carved in ruby and amethyst and emerald, or little ivory sages in lacquered boxes or finely tapestried silken panels woven into fables of the phoenix bird. And one lifts high a wonder work of moon-white jade, wrought into an image of Lord Buddha throned on the lotus, Lord Buddha with eyes fixed in rapture, his right hand extending two fingers to bless the world.

They must be going to the Palace of the mighty King, these gift bearers, attended by eunuchs in dazzling coats, by guards mailed and sworded and terrible, by musicians ringing bells and bearing drums, by hordes of retainers more gorgeous than poppies in the sun. They will turn from the road into a covered walk whose pillared roof, tiled without and painted within, answers with man colours the challenge of the light. Slowly they file between the crimson columns to kneel before the Dragon Throne and lay their gifts around it. The gilded banners salute the sacred roofs of six colours, the roofs orange and green, turquoise and heliotrope, peacock and sapphire, with their little guardian animals at the corners…

(Harriet Munro, *In Cathay*)

⌣⋮⌢

It was in these sumptuous, but charming personal surroundings the old Dowager passed the last years of her life. Tradition says that in this regal setting the Empress Dowager breathed her last and that she died as she had lived, dramatically.

Ill and worn, with a premonition that she was near her end, this indomitable woman courageously rose from her sick bed to give audience to the Dalai Lama. Seated on her throne in hieratic pose and full of ceremonial robes, she impersonated for the last time the dignity and power of her mighty ancestors as the doors were thrown open and the Buddhist Pope, in his gorgeous yellow vestments entered and bowed before her.

But the long silence was broken by a deep sigh. The proud head fell back. The terrified eunuchs scattered. All feared this sudden tragedy yet none dared verify their fears. Finally the Dalai Lama himself mounted the dais and confirmed them. A way of life for a great nation had ended.

*I*N THOSE DAYS AFTER THEIR arrival in Peking, General Horvath was always busy. He took no part in the daily happy exuberance of his family. But all the rest were having a wonderful time—and I was, too!

The only thing was—they always moved as a bunch. It seemed impossible to detach Doushka from the others. When I suggested this, that or the other idea for morning's amusement it way always agreed to with alacrity—but they all came along! It wasn't a conspiracy, it was just the way they lived. They did everything together and very often their mother came too!

In a way Mama was more fun than her daughters. She always organised them. It was she who made sure they had their sketching things. These they always carried everywhere and, at any moment the whole party would stop, look about them. Was there a good 'view' from here? If there was, whatever the destination, it was put off, forgotten. They must sketch. They were absolutely caught by the moment.

At first this made me very irritated. I was always impatient, obsessed with the idea of getting there, wherever 'there' might be—and being alone with Doushka. But it never worked out like that. They were quite unhurried. Time was of no account whatever. There was always tomorrow. So, slowly they got me trained.

It was, after all, very pleasant to sit about with them, so busy and content, silent, absorbed, with their sketching. It gave me the chance to sit next to Doushka and pretend I was interested in her view of the subject. I was never allowed to touch her. If I laid my hand on her shoulder it was at once brushed off, with a little smile—the family was watching. Russian words passed between the sisters. What were they saying? Encouraging her? Laughing at me? I felt shut out—but it didn't seem to matter.

I remember one day finding our way out to a little temple I had seen, not far out from the city, but quite in the country, abandoned, as many of these beautiful small temples were, with no monks any more to tend them, but leaving, like some aroma of past holiness, such an atmosphere of peace and love, it was marvellous.

It affected the girls too. They were silent, just being there. They had come on their own that day—I suppose Mum had decided she could trust me—all three crowding into my old car which was a two-seater, but you could squeeze in four, using the dickey. Now I could see they were wildly happy just at finding this secret place and enjoying it.

Ninka, the youngest, who was also the most intelligent and had even got a word or two of English, suddenly stopped and looked at me:

'Lewis! You could marry Doushka here!'

It made us all laugh. It was such a ridiculous idea. But Ninka wasn't to be put off.

'Why not? It's holy here. Better than in a church.'

Mimi and Doushka said nothing. Mimi was evidently shocked into silence. Doushka, eyes downcast, was fishing out her sketching things. I didn't say anything either. I was quite shocked too. I was full of love, but marriage… that was quite a new, quite a different idea.

They started their sketching. I sat down by Doushka, as I always did. Neither of us said anything.

⌣∶∾

Ninka had started something. I loved this beautiful creature, so close to me and yet so far away, worshipped or desired, yet somehow not to be touched, I was bemused. I didn't know what to do. I couldn't say why… I wanted to gaze at her, hold her, possess her—if it would ever be allowed—always have her by me, like a picture, a jewel, a keepsake for life.

For Life? I didn't bother about life. I didn't think of it as something you could 'have'. It was just 'there', something you lived in, full of surprises, beauties, mysteries, challenges, just put there to be met, dealt with and left—like scenery, scenery in a car—that was it. Life was my scenery, edible scenery, to be grabbed and gulped down! Love me, love my scenery. Come with me, enjoy it all as much as I do, follow me wherever it takes you. If you're with me, it'll be all right. I don't know how—but it will, just take my word for it. I'm your lucky star!

That was the way I thought about it, then. It never even occurred to me that anyone sensible could think about things in any other way but my way. Then was the world full of fools who didn't think my way?—Well, more or less, yes: that's what it amounted to.

But be practical. You have to eat. You have to have a home for this jewel of yours. Have you put anything by, have you any savings, any job, any safe job, how will you manage? Have your parents any money, can they help?…

No, no, no, no! Don't worry! Don't think about things like that. I don't care about money. I live my life, from moment to moment. Tomorrow will bring what tomorrow brings. Why should I worry about it? I have to meet it—that's all. Grab the moment! That's the point. Never miss the moment. And it'll come out all right. You'll see…

I write all this in my old age—with a cat on my knee—in a blessed detachment of peace and happiness. I have lived like this. The risks, the mistakes, the losses, the gains—they are all there. Up and down. In and out. In a wonderful, exciting, marvellous life! People call it 'being lucky'. But you have to bring something to life to be lucky. You have to make your contribution. And it's in the Bible, after all ... 'Take no thought for the morrow. For the morrow will take thought for the things of itself ...'

Anyway that was how I thought then, lived then—but of course I didn't write it all down and justify it, as I do now. I just gulped it down!

And most of it I can't remember. Time slipped past us like the scent of lilies, the taste of honey and ice-cream!

There was even a little row! I got tired of always being pushed away by this tempting, tantalising, keep-away-idol whom I was never allowed to touch, to kiss. Very well, I decided, I would push off, find another girl, amuse myself. It took a week. Then came a note:

'Darling. It's all because I am so terribly, terribly shy. I can't help it. Help me. Forgive me. Come back to me, I love you.'

That was her vow. And it was a love vow—taken for life. I didn't know or understand it—then. It was love, given from a pure young heart. For me. For life. For ever. And I accepted it easily, thoughtlessly. I hadn't the least idea of what it meant. I hadn't depths like that. I couldn't feel like that. When, years and years later, one dreadful day, when I woke up to it, to all it had meant to her, to her broken, empty life, I was disgusted, horrified. How trivial, thoughtless, utterly selfish had all my 'love' been! How, worthless. What a fake I was. It set a black cross of egoism on my life. Nothing can wipe it out or make it good. What is the payment for a 'do it yourself' life?

⌣∶∾

Well, whatever it is, Doushka has more than paid her share of it, struggling with her own life, her own gains and losses, her own ins and outs, to emerge, in old age, magically free from anxiety, having picked a plum from the pickle, steady and engaging and very much master of her faculties and her life situations.

We have agreed that neither of us have any idea of how those days, almost a year, went by when we were promised to each other. There was a time when I was sick with some fever, there was even a family seaside holiday at TsingTao, there were summer thunderstorms and winter snows, but probably the best way to get the flavour of those days would be to pick on a few moments, here and there, which seem to have retained the burnished flavour of a dream past looked at through my ropey old telescope a lifetime later.

We'd taken in the great sights, temples, palaces, monuments, all the highlights that made the noble background to the colour and taste of a unique city. What picked out our days later were the incidentals, a sandstorm, a downpour, that week of thunderous heat, that day we happened to be in Lantern St. in a sudden windstorm.

The Chinese had the good idea of putting each of their common trades into its own street. Thus there was Shoe St. where you could buy all kinds of footwear from straw sandals to wooden boots, or Fashion St. where the girls found mouth watering materials from cottons to brocades. Here we one day happened to notice, in English, written on a piece of cardboard pinned to a dress from a dealer eager for foreign custom: 'Ladies get fits upstairs'!

Then there was China St. and Furniture St.: all these were part of the Chinese City outside the walls of Peking itself, but the heart of the everyday life of the capital. The narrow streets were bursting with every kind of buying and selling and always exciting, teeming with people, gay, noisy, shouting with life—a supermarket, fifty years ahead of its time.

That day in Lantern St. the sun was filtering through a sloping narrow lane where hundreds of lanterns were hanging, swaying, swinging, hung on wire above people's heads. Below them were the tiny hovels where dozens of craftsmen were creating out of paper and bamboo these featherweight bubbles of gaiety and happiness—but, alas, not designed for gales!

When the freak squall suddenly struck, it was pandemonium. The lantern owners—and the public—rushed at these runaway jewels to save them. The whole street was a whirl of airborne lanterns flying away in a gorgeous cavalcade of colour. The huge square ones, big as a beehive, with coloured panels and gilded roofs, blew into the air like mad balloons, bronze monsters that pulled out like dragons, slid over the roof tops like serpents, hundreds of small gold moons, built to house a candle, disappeared like lost planets. Away went the lanterns for weddings, funerals, feastdays, parties—in a moment the whole street had disappeared. Then suddenly silence. The squall had gone by like a wild monster. We both stood there bewildered, silent, a boy was crying. The work of months had gone! People talked about it for weeks.

The day long clang and clatter of Copper St. was quite a different matter. Conversation was impossible. The deafening beating of hammers drowned everything. It was a broad open street with the world's traffic going up and down before the big open booths where half naked sweaty young men with hammers seemed bent on smashing acres of copper sheet into every possible household article you could imagine. In those days copper was the everyday working stuff of all China and the rhythms of the hammers would have been heaven to any modern composer. There were the light ones with their high pitched rattle, busy making trays or buckets or spittoons, over them came the mezzos with their heavy regular beat working in couples on big cauldrons or barrels. Under it all boomed the double bass of stone-headed bashers whose roars drowned the rumble of the waggons and the shouts of carters calling on the watermen to spread their cooling stuff from wicker ladles to lay the choking dust. 'Gosh! They love work!' I said.

It was compulsive to walk down the hot, noisy street. It gave a lusty feeling of China at work, all carried on in the open. Everyone could see what his neighbour was doing and this seemed to give life to the whole community. All these craftsmen and carters must know each other. They were partners in a rough and ready way who laboured at peace with one another. There was a feeling that all was well with this shouting swearing struggling world of men. This was how it ought to be, everybody fighting for his place but none a stranger to his neighbour.

Doushka echoed my thought: 'They're alive! And happy!— like us!'

ᴥᴥ

One morning we were walking in HaTaMen Avenue, the main easterly north-south avenue of Peking. It was, as usual, a crowd of rickshaws, carts, waggons, all the rough and tumble of daily life rattling by. But then a smart little brougham caught our attention.

The brougham was—in case you have forgotten—the luxury vehicle of the Victorian age. It was a small black box with a shiny roof, doors on either side, big bright yellow wheels and a driver, sitting on the roof. It was the luxury carriage of the age, tarted up, painted, varnished and polished like a jewel and was pulled by one of those small Mongolian ponies that were driven down from the north every winter in flocks to be sold in Peking. Some of those ponies were beautiful and bought by young Legation sportsmen as their polo mounts.

As these ponies were small, little bigger than donkeys, the Peking broughams had been scaled down to suit their size. It also suited the size of their owners who, then, were small men.

The whole turn-out looked like a new toy, the emblem of luxury and wealth.

But later, when I was there, a curious case of one-upmanship had occurred. Some enterprising importer had introduced the Australian Whaler to Peking. The Australian Whaler was a gaunt full-sized horse with a dejected air. But it was a novelty and it had become the 'thing' for the rich to have one to pull their broughams. But the rump of the whaler was higher than the roof of the brougham it pulled and the driver was obliged to sit on top of it all. The grotesque circus-like effect was irresistibly ridiculous.

So we laughed as we saw this monstrosity come by. The whaler trotted along at twice the speed of the other traffic with the brougham bouncing wildly on the non-existent road. Then, of course—it had to happen—off came the right hand wheel! The coachman was thrown into the gutter. The brougham lay on its side and the wheel, with a life of its own, went skipping off along the street. Disaster!

But what had happened to the occupant, the great man who had now suffered such a loss of face it would take years to live it down? Slowly somebody was pushing open the top door of the brougham. A small elderly man's head appeared, immaculately dressed, perfectly unruffled. He stood there, looking lost, surprised and angry, clutching the open door, balancing himself, surveying the wreck—and fanning himself. He was small, neat and absolutely master of the situation. People appeared to carry some of his things. A rickshaw was called, he gave some orders. His people would deal with the unfortunate mess. Then he rolled off, flipping away the slight mishap with a dismissive gesture of his fan. That, we thought is the way a Chinese aristocrat keeps his dignity in emergency.

*M*Y FRONT LINE FLYING ON THE Somme and the casual life and death values in war had blotted out my feelings about religion. My father's white surplice on the Sunday pulpits of my youth belonged to childhood. So when Easter came round and the Horvath family were in great spirits, making ready to celebrate this, the most sacred moment in their Christian year, I felt quite unmoved by it all and even reluctant to go to the Russian service, which I knew was long and emotional. I had seen too much death at close quarters to have much belief in the Resurrection and my logical scientific schooling didn't leave much room for fairy tales. But, of course I had to go, I was part of their family after all and Doushka took it as a matter of course that I should go with her.

So we bought our candles and crowded into the little Russian church. I was surprised by how many Russians there were in Peking. Soon I became engulfed in the solemnity and beauty of the service, by the dignity and beauty of the Priest's robes and, above all, by the depths of the chanting which seemed physically to touch something in my heart and, as it were, opened my soul to God. Suddenly all my childhood came back. I remembered how my father had given his life to religion and had never sought to influence me and how I had quite ignored all that side of my life. Now I knew, as my father had known, that I must always make place for it.

So, I was ready, when the time came, to light my candle from Doushka's and join in the procession, made by the whole congregation, to circle the church with our candles lit, searching for the body of Jesus on the night after his Crucifixion. The choir preceded us invoking Him and we followed slowly, silently, my heart somehow overcome by the wonder of so many others transformed by such faith, such hope, that somehow we could find Him.

At last we returned to the big door by which we had left. It was locked. We were shut out and crowded up around it.

After a long silence the young priest who had led us ventured up to the door and knocked on it. It was opened and a figure stood there with a raised Crucifix in one hand and an open palm of blessing in the other, saying:

'Christ is risen!'

A murmur, half tear, half joy, ran through all of us and we turned to each other repeating the miracle: 'Christ is risen,' 'Christ is risen!', and then, so overcome, we all started kissing each other and laughing with joy—and the sort of happiness that only comes once in a lifetime.

⌣∶∼

I don't remember the formalities of our engagement. I don't remember proposing—though Doushka told me, 70 years later, I had done the right thing, asking her to be my bride under a beautiful flowering cherry tree! I am sure I must have asked the permission of my parents-in-law; but what I remember best is what was now freely given, the licence, so to speak, of being allowed to wander about, alone, together, where we wanted, on our own.

I wanted to make Doushka an engagement present and thought that a visit to Kingfisher-Feather St. would be the place to find something special. It was a secluded hutung in the Chinese city, narrow, small and somehow secret. Only a few shops had their screens raised to display their wares. The men who smiled at the passer-by were discreet, neatly dressed in their long pale blue gowns from neck to ankle and gave the impression, something like Asprey's, that they were not really there to sell anything and it was even quite an honour if they smile at you.

All this exclusivity was justified in what they had to sell. They were a small group of artists specialising in the most delicate jewels I have ever seen—bangles, brooches, ear-rings, hair combs, all framed in cradles of silver and inlaid with king-fisher feathers. The dark blue lustre of these rare beauties flashed and shone from their glittering beds with an exquisite delicate beauty. They laid them out for us to see and, as if to explain what they were, produced a stuffed kingfisher, proudly displayed on its silver stand.

Doushka picked up the bird and looked at it.

'How do they get the feathers?' she asked.

I didn't know. I didn't speak enough Chinese to ask. 'I sup-pose they catch them and pluck the feathers,' I said.

'Kill them you mean?' she asked.

'I suppose so.'

She put down the brooch she was looking at.

'They are beautiful' she said. 'But'—with such a look—'please, my darling—let's go somewhere else. I want a ring!'

The salesman put the things away. I suppose he thought we couldn't afford them.

A ring! Why hadn't I thought of it? Because anybody could have a ring, and I wanted her to have something nobody else had!

But this was her day. The ring shop was crowded. Everybody was busy buying rings! I felt awkward doing such a personal, private thing in public! But Doushka was ferreting about. Soon she saw and picked up a small neat ring with five small diamonds surrounded with a garland of tiny amethysts.

When the salesman saw it on her beautiful slender fingers, he clapped his hands, quite entranced. In those days Chinese girls had small, rather dumpy hands. He held onto her hands, gazing at them reverently, as if they were a work of art—which they were.

It was a moment of great joy for her. I remember we walked away from the shop, my hand in her lovely hand. She was radiantly happy.

~:~

The idea of marrying Doushka had only come up when the days of timeless happiness of being on cloud nine were over. Discussing practical matters seemed an intrusion, besides raising all sorts of day to day problems. Marriage, of course; but when? Now or later? And where? Russian or English? Would a Russian marriage in China be legal in England? Then dates, receptions, clothes, etc., etc. Visits to Harbin for a wedding dress. In Russia the Horvath standing was such that everything would have to be done in grand style. In China, thank heaven, we could keep it simple.

Then there was my own job problem, the Chinese contract was only for one year. It could be renewed, but did I want that? Was there any future in teaching the Chinese to fly? China didn't seem ready or organised for it. On the commercial side, flying was still a dream. The practical problems of setting up Chinese air services seemed years away. The Vimy passenger aircraft we had brought were a waste of money.

Obviously being English, I should return to my own country, but there was a pull to stay in China. I had grown fond of the Chinese and their way of life. But there seemed no way one could make a career in Peking. In the UK at least I spoke the language. I supposed I could find something to do. But what? I had absolutely no idea of how to make a living. I had just been 'cannon fodder' really. Well taught—up to the age of 16. But the

War had put a full stop to any idea of the future—for millions, alas, there was none.

So I was really uneducated and in no way prepared for life. Those vital years, from 17 to 20 had been lost. I didn't like the idea of going back to University. I had been too much in life to go back to study. But I don't remember ever having the least doubt that everything was bound to turn out all right. I had absolute faith in myself. I didn't really face the future, the chances I was taking for Doushka or for myself. If fools step in, angels will guard them. That was my philosophy.

So I decided we must return to England and that was quite a job in itself. There was all the treasure I had collected in my little house and wanted to take with me. All that had to be sorted, chairs, tables, chests, what to take and not to take and all the arrangements for packing and shipping. Then there was giving up the house, getting a British Passport for Doushka, booking tickets for Shanghai, getting berths on a ship, and so on—to say nothing of the money.

Then there was Jo, my house boy, who had looked after me ever since the first day I had met him in the hotel. I was devoted to him. He was the first—and I think, the only personal servant I have ever had in my life. How to reward him, help him, what would become of him? I remember him when we finally left and our train moved out of the station, seeing him there on the platform, in deep distress, clasping both hands to his heart and throwing them out to me, time and time again. Dear faithful devoted Jo. He knew we should never see each other again.

All these were emotional as well as practical crises and upset me more than I knew at the time. But I think I must have known, subconsciously, it was a turning point in our lives and it haunted me. Later, when I could look more objectively I saw how terribly young we were. My whole life had been dominated by my war experience; hers by a rich memory of an idyllic childhood. We had absolutely nothing in common. It could not possibly succeed. Yet we were so certain that it would we never gave failure a thought.

On October 19th, 1920 we were married. The depth and warmth of the chanting, the robes of the priests, the incense, the solemnity of the occasion, the gold crowns held above our heads as we circled the altar, above all the beauty of my bride, to whom this was the most wonderful moment of her life, all this went over me in a sort of dreamy blur. I had jaundice and was physically so low that I had to be helped up by my 'best man' during the ceremony. But it all must have been a crisis that disappeared once the die had been cast and the decisions taken. I remember nothing of the great wedding party that was held afterwards.

It took me many, many years to 'see myself', my self-justification. The selfishness, the thoughtlessness of my life never entered my head at the time. I had taken my bride absolutely for granted. I was, in fact, abducting a girl of 18, brought up like a princess, into a faraway country where she didn't speak the language, would have no family nor a single friend. I never thought about what sort of life she would lead or the conditions she would have to accept or what the future might hold for her. In fact she had to face problems of everyday life that would have daunted an ordinary English girl, bred to it, with some anxiety. But I don't think she ever thought about it. She just accepted and faced everything because of her absolute trust and love for me—what else had she to depend on?—and I consistently failed in all my obligations.

However I am determined not to let the remorse of the future darken the very real joy and happiness of those two years of roses, roses that we spent together in China. I wanted her to have all a gay young man could give to his beautiful young wife. And we were happy as, I think, only the very young can be happy.

'Darling' she said, very shyly, at a moment when there were other impulses, 'I would like to keep myself ... to myself ... until we are married, so as to have God's blessing on our love.'

We had, as it happened, a double marriage, for Mimi, the eldest Horvath daughter, was marrying a Russian Count (with whom she left for Canada and was to live happily for a lifetime with him) and we took our vows together. Now all the arrangements were made, all the dates fixed and we set out to spend our honeymoon in one of the oldest and most beautiful temples in China—Chieh T'ai Ssu.

The Great Bell at Chieh T'ai Ssu

I HAD ALREADY VISITED TEMPLES BEFORE, so I had some idea of what it meant. Going off into the 'wilds' of China—as they then were—was quite an undertaking. In those days it was done in style. Everything, but everything, had to be taken with us.

I still have a vivid memory of our departure from a Peking siding in an open coal truck, which was being loaded with endless chests containing clothes, kitchen things, groceries, glass and china, food and wine, linen, cushions, chairs, a table and two large mattresses. All this had been organised by the faithful and extremely competent 'boy', Jo. I had had nothing to do with it. He and my cook and coolie were heaving the stuff up into the truck and shouting at each other and two other train porters who had joined in. The problem of getting the 'tai-tai' (Doushka) aboard was solved by the sudden appearance of a step-ladder and all the rest of us swarmed on board and Jo, always treating the tai-tai like a jewel, after asking my permission, shouted at the engine driver.

I have still no idea where this 'train' came from. It had an incredibly old and clapped-out engine and one truck. Had Papa, as erstwhile commander of all the railways in China, caused it to appear as a sort of wedding present to his daughter? If so he might have done better! Anyway the engine blew out black smoke and cinders, its whistle screeched and the whole thing suddenly lurched forward throwing us to the dirty, dusty floor of the truck and, in a series of glorious superhuman puffs, chugged out of the Peking siding.

What line we were on, where it led to, will remain for ever a mystery. All I had said to Jo was that I wanted to go to Chieh T'ai Ssu and given him the date. He had come back a couple of days later saying, 'Master, Chieh T'ai Ssu, all fixed!' You can hardly believe that things could be that easy, but, somehow or other in those days, it was so.

Anyhow, ridiculously happy in an altogether crazy and uncomfortable situation, our eyes and hair full of smoke and flying ashes, we bumped off gaily into nowhere. I have no idea where the line went, nor what was the station at which we were to stop and unload all that tackle we had taken such a sweat to onload.

After a couple of hours of this, the whistle blew again and we lurched to a stop at a place, I was told, was the nearest we could get to the Temple. The rest (four hours) we should walk. Our stop was, as far as I could see, no more than an open place, golden hills and blue sky, where we could jump to the ground either side of the track. But we were evidently expected for the truck was immediately assailed by an eager crowd of excited shouting Chinese donkey boys actively demanding our custom.

Swarming into the truck, dozens of them hurled all our chests and possessions wildly overboard. Chaos reigned. But actually the men knew their business very well. Nothing was spoiled or damaged and soon there was Jo bargaining and arguing about the choice of donkeys and setting up our caravan.

Doushka, I remember, watched all the hubbub with a sort of detached amusement, brushing the cinders out of her glorious hair. She could never have seen anything like it in her life—and nor had I. Jo had provided her with a chair and I stood by her. There certainly had never been a start to a honeymoon like this—and never would be again.

There then appeared out of the shed eight coolies and two large chairs. Jo had insisted, against my wish, that it was quite unsuitable for two 'young lords', as he put it, to walk on this, so special journey to 'look-see God'. Each chair had two long saplings bound onto it, one on each side, and four young coolies took up the ends of the saplings on their shoulders. The whole contraption was then lifted high into the air onto the coolies' shoulders and we were to sit in the chairs and be carried to the Temple.

Two hundred years ago it was common for the rich to go everywhere in 'sedan' chairs, but somehow I felt uncomfortable being carried by other men. Doushka was frankly frightened to death of the whole thing. 'I have no balance. I shall fall off' she kept saying. But the chairs were set down by us and we were invited to sit in them and 'try' them.

Meanwhile the caravan of about 25 donkeys had been loaded with all our gear. The Chinese donkey was a very small, lean and incredibly tough animal, carrying heavy loads without complaint. Their owners were evidently very fond of them and decorated their ankles with bracelets of tiny bells. Now, waiting the order to start, they looked irresistibly comical in their extraordinary loads, cooking stoves, washtubs and mattresses would obviously fall off their narrow backs. However, at a shout, the whole caravan set out in triumphant single file, each donkey making a gay jangle of bracelet music in the dust and the boys shouting encouraging swearwords at them: Prrrup! Prrrup! So we set off into the Chinese afternoon.

There was something wonderful, very exciting, about that moment. Where were we going? It was an adventure, the start of something, strange, happy, very much our own, belonging to our time, our youth, our future and towards a Temple which would leave, I believed in some subconscious way, an imprint on our lives. Such are the dreams of youth. We are permitted to be romantic at twenty-two.

By now Doushka was laughing. Once over the nervousness of looking at life six feet above the ground we had both got used to this springy swaying way of travel. It became wonderfully comfortable and we could look over the whole caravan as it kept up its fast walking pace. After two hours we stopped under the shade of trees at an old group of tombs where Jo brewed us boiling tea, the best thing, he assured us for hot weather.

The rolling open farming country then gave way to hills. We could just make out on the horizon the outline of walls of Peking on the eastern horizon. We turned into long valleys with dried-up, stony stream beds, then to narrow gorges with steep over-hanging 'Chinese-picture' vistas. There began to be a sort of wonder in the landscape. We felt we were nearing something, quite close, above us.

We stopped at a tiny village. The people looked at us with stone eyes as we got down from the chairs to walk up the long flights of steps that led to the gate of the Temple.

We left our chairs in the village. They would be there to take us back. All the rest of the caravan laboured up the endless steps to the open place before the Temple Gate. Here there was a mêlée of unloading, since no animals are allowed within the gates of the Temple. But the boys disappeared one by one, each carrying a load up to the guest quarters within the Temple.

'Now' said Jo, pointing, 'Ring bell. Say friends arrive.' He was pointing to a small *Tingah* which stood on the edge of this open place with a glorious view down the valley up which we had just climbed. A *Tingah* is a sort of small summer house. This one had a green tiled curling roof standing on four pillars and from the roof hung a huge bronze bell, about five feet high. On one side, hanging on chains was a heavy log, a tree trunk. Pull it back and let go! It struck the skirt of the bell.

Boom! It called, ringing out strong and clear. We stood listening to the dying note, echoing away over the hills. There was a wonderful feeling about having done it! I kissed my

twenty-four-hour-old wife! No doubt about it: we had arrived at
Chieh T'ai Ssu.

‿⁚∾

A Buddhist Temple is always open and ready to receive visitors.
Because Chieh T'ai Ssu was the favourite retreat of the great
Emperor Ch'ien Lung everything in the Temple was built on a
noble and lavish scale. The guest courtyard stood at the end of
the main Terrace, four pavilions built, as the Chinese always
build, on the four sides of an open square, ample and beautifully proportioned.

Before the front room was a deep veranda and on this, and
the room behind, we set out our things. Jo put up his cooking
stove in the open at the far end of the courtyard and all the boys
cooked and slept in the back room. He quickly set up our
folding table and chairs. The cook found spring water and
brought us a jug of it, cool and refreshing. We were glad to relax
after the turmoil of the day. I remember how we just sat, hardly
talking, already bewitched by the silence and peace of the place.
Doushka had been in temples before, but this was something
else and I hoped she would feel it as I did.

An hour later, a very tall and dignified monk appeared and
stood before us, in his rich golden robe, bowing. We both got
up and returned the bow and I tentatively held out my hand, not
knowing if this was quite the thing to do. However he smiled,
took Doushka's hand and mine. At that moment Jo appeared,
obviously very impressed, bowing again and again. The monk
then spoke to him, quietly and slowly.

When he stopped, Jo turned to us and said: 'This man is top
man, Master here. He say glad you come to Buddha house. You
friends. You can look-see all temples. But not to go where
monks pray.'

I told Jo to thank him and tell him we would obey him and, after another bow, the monk, whom we later realised was the Abbot of the Temple, suddenly pulled something from his sleeve. It was a small tin which he offered to Doushka, with another bow. She saw it was a present and took it, smiling and taking his hand again. The Abbot formally withdrew his hand, bowed and walked away.

As soon as he was out of sight we looked excitedly at his present, this curious tin. The label was half torn off, but it was Japanese and read, in English, 'Japanese Lychees'! This was our welcome to Chieh T'ai Ssu.

Sitting on our veranda, the main terrace lay on our left, a long shaded vista, dominated by a huge white pine, and as broad as a country road. This gave scale to the whole place. It was a large group of temples on different levels above and below us. Along the terrace, on our right, over a low wall we could see roofs and courtyards of temples below, with their decorated eaves and hanging wind-rung bells. On the left stood the main temple and beyond it others we could explore. All this lay absolutely silent in the evening light.

'As if there was nobody here' said Doushka.

'They say there are more than a hundred monks.'

'A hundred! What are they doing?'

'Training to be priests, I believe.'

'It's like a sort of college then?'

'Ch'ien Lung endowed it to be the Buddhist University of north China.'

Doushka seemed to think this over. 'It frightens me, a bit' she laughed, shyly.

'Darling! It's one of the holiest, most sacred places in China.'

'Is that why you brought me here?'

'I'd never thought of it, but yes, I suppose it is, in a way.'

'Why?'

'A sort of top note to start on, darling.'

She took my hand, 'I love you' she said.

I kissed her. 'I want it to be something so different, so outside life, that it can be a sort of dream to come back to. I want us to have it to remember.'

'I shall remember.'

'Let's go and ask the old Buddha's blessing. He's here, only next door' I laughed.

We walked along the terrace, it was only a few yards. There, on our left stood a beautiful double roof higher than all the others. The tall doors were open. We took the few steps up onto a higher terrace. And stood. And looked.

This image of the Buddha seemed huge, twice, three times life size. His bulk seemed immense, overpowering. The symbol of love, peace, understanding, he sat there on his thousand leaved lotus whose petals curled up, like a divine dais. On the tip of every petal stood a minute image of Himself, begging all men to remember Him in every corner of the world.

Trivial thoughts burst out over the awe of just looking at Him. He must have been built in the open and the roof round him; how could he look so clean, so fresh as if he had been made that day. He must be washed and cared for, like a man. Had he been a man, living, in the flesh, all those years ago? Now the holy media had got hold of Him and dragged him down to an advertisement: 'Each man kills the thing he loves.'

Now, when in later years I have come to believe that the Life Force, the Presence of God, inhabits every living thing, it seems to me that there can also be holy places, storerooms, where His Presence lies deep, waiting to be found and that those who have the need are directed towards them, to be blessed, refreshed and fortified by finding there the very Essence of Himself. So, like swimmers, we plunged into this refreshment and whenever we came back to it, we should find the aftertaste in our hearts.

We spent the days exploring. We discovered a temple, full of demons, tortured, grotesque and agonized figures. We found

another full of drums. Another filled with all manner of fit-
ments for ceremonies, bowls, stands for incense burners,
lanterns.

During our first night we were awakened by a sudden roll of
drums. We sat up, listening. Had something happened? Some
danger, some attack, some accident? After a few minutes it
stopped—as suddenly as it had begun.

'I suppose it's all right?' Doushka was alarmed.

'It's to wake the monks up—like us.'

'Well I wish they wouldn't do it at night.'

'Part of the training.'

'I don't understand, darling'—the way she said darling was
delicious—'why do they run after God—when He's here
already?'

'I don't know. But I think they get something out of it.'

What they got was unexpectedly shown us next day when a
small, neat little Chinese introduced himself to us. He was
obviously a monk, but different. He wore a dark green robe
and seemed gay, vivacious, middle-aged, bald and very much
alive, his eyes twinkling, his hands talking. But what amazed us
was his fluent, inaccurate English.

'My name Wang. I was sailor. Got to Cardiff. You know
Cardiff? Very good city. Many Chinese live Cardiff.'

There was something immediately likeable about Wang. He
evidently wanted to talk. It wasn't exactly what we'd expected
at Chieh T'ai Ssu, but here he was, might be interesting—and
his English would help.

'I find God at Penzance.' He came out with this suddenly,
amused at himself and gave a light laugh that seemed part of
him. 'Yes! You think this funny?—not at the time. No sir!' he
laughed again. 'Storm! My old ship turned over. I go too. In
heavy clothes. Don't swim. Thought I would die. Then I
fought death. Prayed. Promised God: if I live I will give my life
to You! Lifeboat saved me, Yes! God gave me another life! So I

came back to China to keep my promise. Worked, studied, became a priest. Now I help boys who work here.'

It was a strange enough story, but while he talked I was looking down on his head, fascinated by the spots on the top of it—nine little scars, arranged in threes.

'How did you get those, Wang?' I asked.

'Ah, yes! You like them?' He laughed again, shortly. 'Very expensive.' His eyes twinkled, but he was serious now. 'It was a penance, a hard penance, necessary to me. Nine small cones of sulphur are stuck to my head. Then they are lit, they burn long time. Ten days it took. Burning out.' He laughed again, quickly, gaily, seemingly to himself, then took our hands, held them. 'That way, remember God—always! Must go!'

We were horrified. He was gone.

How did we spend those days? Now I can't remember. We were just happy, happy together. Doushka was very inquisitive. She liked to look into everything, she found out from Jo that the little ornamental towers, several of them, just below the long wall, were 'stupas', special tombs in which the Abbots were buried upright. She discovered the small hexagon 'summer house', built especially for Ch'ien Lung's meditation. She heard from Jo that the young monks under training lived on one bowl of soup a day for a month. I confess I was lazy. I just liked to sit and drink in the tranquillity, the holiness of the place that seemed to come out of the very air we breathed.

Of course we walked quite a bit, in the woods around, above the walls of the monastery, looking down on the rambling living buildings below us, the wonderful 'full-moon' doorways, the old bronze incense burners. We didn't talk much religion, discuss things, we just lived in the moment, let it all sink in, made love …

But of love I will say nothing, not out of shyness or prudery, but simply because I cannot translate feelings into words. They belong to two different parts of us. Only the greatest poets have been able to translate what we feel into what we say, and they not often. Happiness is a state, lost or found in a word, a gesture, a thought. While we are living it, no need to think of it: when it is over we yearn for it and weep because it has gone.

Towards the end of our stay, we were crossing a big open courtyard below the main terrace when we heard the curious murmur that many men make when they are praying. At the far end of the courtyard was a building with open doors and from this the sound had come. Almost at once after it had ended, monks began to emerge from the temple and to walk in file towards us across the courtyard. We moved back at once off the terrace and watched them. They were chanting quietly in time with their steps. Once the file had reached the edge of the terrace right above us, it turned back on itself towards the doors out of which other monks were emerging. This endless file of more than a hundred young men, snaking back and forth finally filled the whole terrace. Seemingly hypnotized, eyes closed, with expressionless faces, they all slowly re-entered the temple. We saw Wang, our green robed friend, standing, watching the last to go in.

There was a long silence, then a thin single note of a high pitched bell and a sort of gasp, as a hundred men prostrated themselves. The bell rang again. Again that terrible sound. Three times this was repeated. Then the ceremony was over. The monks emerged in couples (some women, we were after-wards told among them) following each other, crossed the courtyard, like dumb, expressionless zombies and disappeared.

I was shocked, moved, something in me revolted at the blind severity of it all. I hadn't realized then, that holiness was a discipline. You have to pay, suffer, to find God.

WE WERE SITTING TOGETHER. It was our last evening. I was feeling sad. I don't like the end of things. I suppose Doushka felt the same, but she never shows anything. The moths were circling our paraffin lamp. The drums were rolling out their evening warning. Wang arrived suddenly, as he always did, smiling, always seemingly full of energy.

After greeting,

'You have been happy here?' he asked.

'Yes, very' I paused, 'But there are some things…'

'Ah! You heard the beating last night?' He asked quickly, anxiously. There had been terrible blows, cries of agony. Awful.

'Yes. What was it?'

'They are young men, boys mostly. It is the end of training. They are tired, it is very hard. A boy was caught smoking. If they tell me, I must throw him out. No way can smoke. So they beat him up. That way I don't know. He can stay—not lose three years training.'

'Seems a funny way to find God—as you call it.'

He laughed merrily. 'You know a better?'

I hesitated. 'I don't like violence.'

'God sent me a storm. Nearly did for me. I promised myself to Him then. Maybe this is boy's storm.'

Again his sudden laughter, 'You see! God very funny chap. Always reminding you! But tonight other way round! Very good family coming to remind God to remember them!' This was obviously tiptop hilarity. 'Yes! Their father gone on long journey, so they come to send prayers and love. Cheer him up!'

Again the laughter. 'Very good chap. All the family cheer! You see. Come. Bring chairs. Sit here. Sit on terrace.'

It was extraordinary how he had foreseen everything, arranged everything, taken us over. We found ourselves doing just as he said, sitting, relaxed, almost drugged by the magic of night in the place, which, under the great brooding Buddha, had somehow changed from 'everyday' into something deep, silent and sacred.

We saw a number of shadows moving towards the centre of the terrace where a bronze scrolled vessel stood, low, square, as big as a bath. A priest in an orange robe came and started scattering gold and white discs into the bronze ('Prayers', said Wang, 'Go up!'). Two other priests seemed to be tying something onto the trees. All three carried lighted tapers, flickering as they moved, and lit the faces of what we now know was to be a whole family, mother and children, come to offer their prayers. They looked happy, almost gay, waving to Wang, who greeted them like old friends.

Then the Abbot appeared, holding a book and began chanting. The whole family froze, kneeling round the cauldron and the friend at our elbow whispered. 'This your present. Take away with you. This remind you of God!'

No sooner had he said this then one priest dipped his taper into the cauldron and the golden discs caught fire. At the same moment the two other priests put their tapers to those hangings on the trees. They were long skeins of Chinese crackers and they went off into exciting bursts of sputtering explosions! Suddenly there was pandemonium. The whole scene was flooded with flames and deafened with machine gun fire. The family prostrated themselves again and again. The temple eaves glowed vermilion and green with flaming, rising prayers. The old Buddha smiled above it all. Then, after a brilliant moment, the last cracker fired and the whole scene, blazing for a moment like a movie set, switched off, died out, smoke drifting through the trees, and the Temple returned to the contemplative silence of the night.

We sat silent, exhausted by this sudden burning jewel of devotion. But our strange friend was ecstatic, clapping his hands with glee. 'You see! Plenty prayers go up! What you think? Impossible God sleep through that racket! God wake up! Help us all.'

Then he suddenly changed, looked at us, his eyes laughing, full of love. 'This remind you of Chieh T'ai Ssu, eh?' He was close to us, intimate. 'This you take away with you. This your reminder of God.'

It was the moment of departure. We were standing by the main gate, on the open space, at the other side of which hung the Great Bell. The donkeys had been loaded and started on their return trip. Jo had left our quarters as we found them, tidy and spotless. Now he stood by us. 'You find chairs in village, Master.'

I couldn't find any Chinese words to thank him. Doushka took his hand in both of hers.

'Jo, you very very good boy,' she said, lamely.

'Master happy, Tai-tai happy. I happy.' He smiled, turned to go, then turned back. 'Maybe Tai-tai ring Goodbye bell? Bring good luck to us all.' He had taken a great fancy to Doushka and smiled at her again and ran off down the steps.

We were alone. I took my wife in my arms and kissed her. Held onto her. A long time.

This was the end of the dream. But we didn't know it, see it. Easy to be romantic, sentimental and fake a happy note to close on. But that's not for us. Both of us have been through it. She through a life of unsatisfied love, saved from all bitterness by her constancy and purity of heart. I, through what? Looking for the future, missing the present? Taking swipes at God with my butterfly net.

'Time for the Bell' I said.

'How do I do it?'

'Pull it right back—and let go.'

The Great Bell boomed away, its note echoing on and on and on...

Even today, at ninety-two and ninety-eight, we are still alive to hear it, meet, take hands once more before a last goodbye, laughing, as we can now, at the joys and sorrows of life and the innocence of love in youth, in 1921.